I0391146

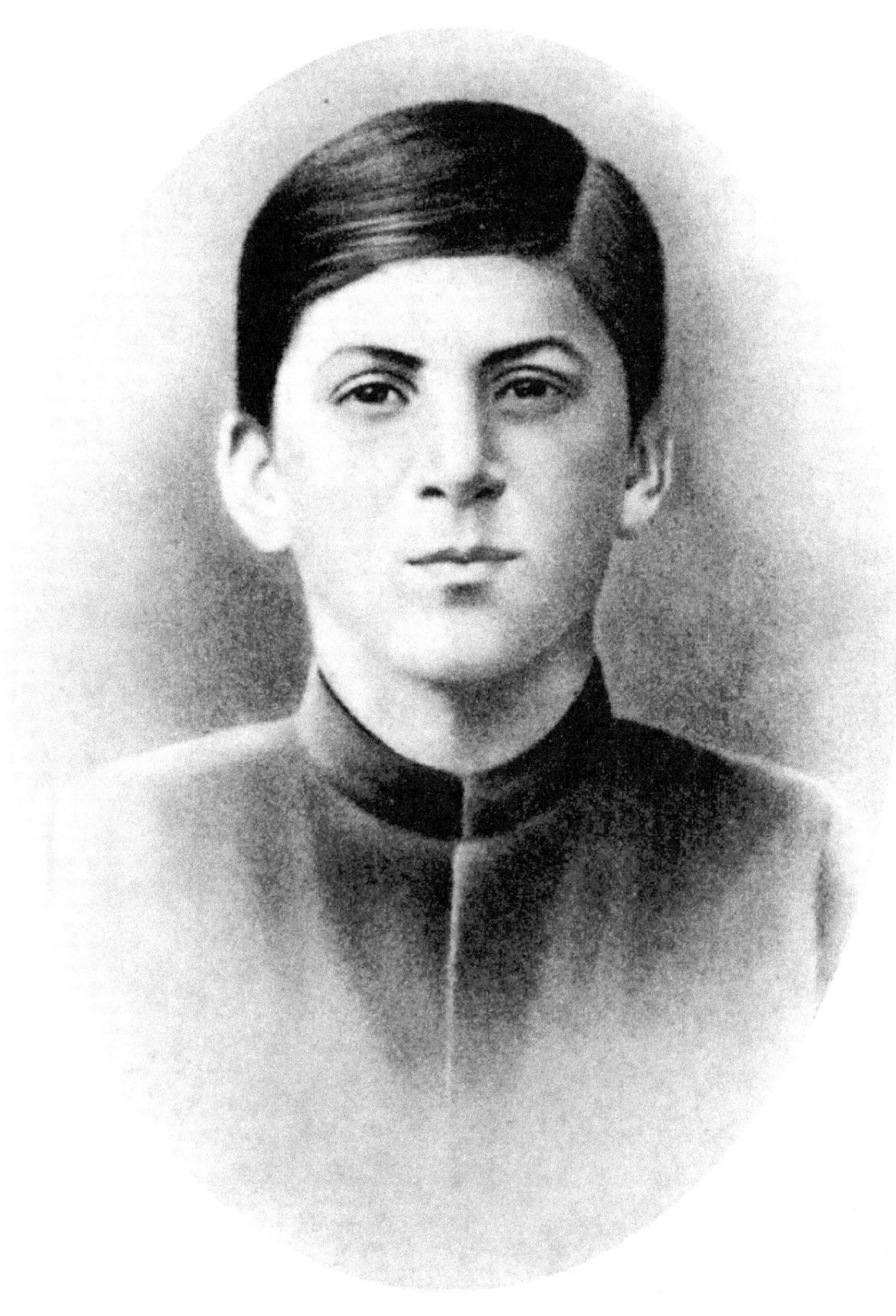

J.W. STALIN
Foto 1894

Stalin (15)

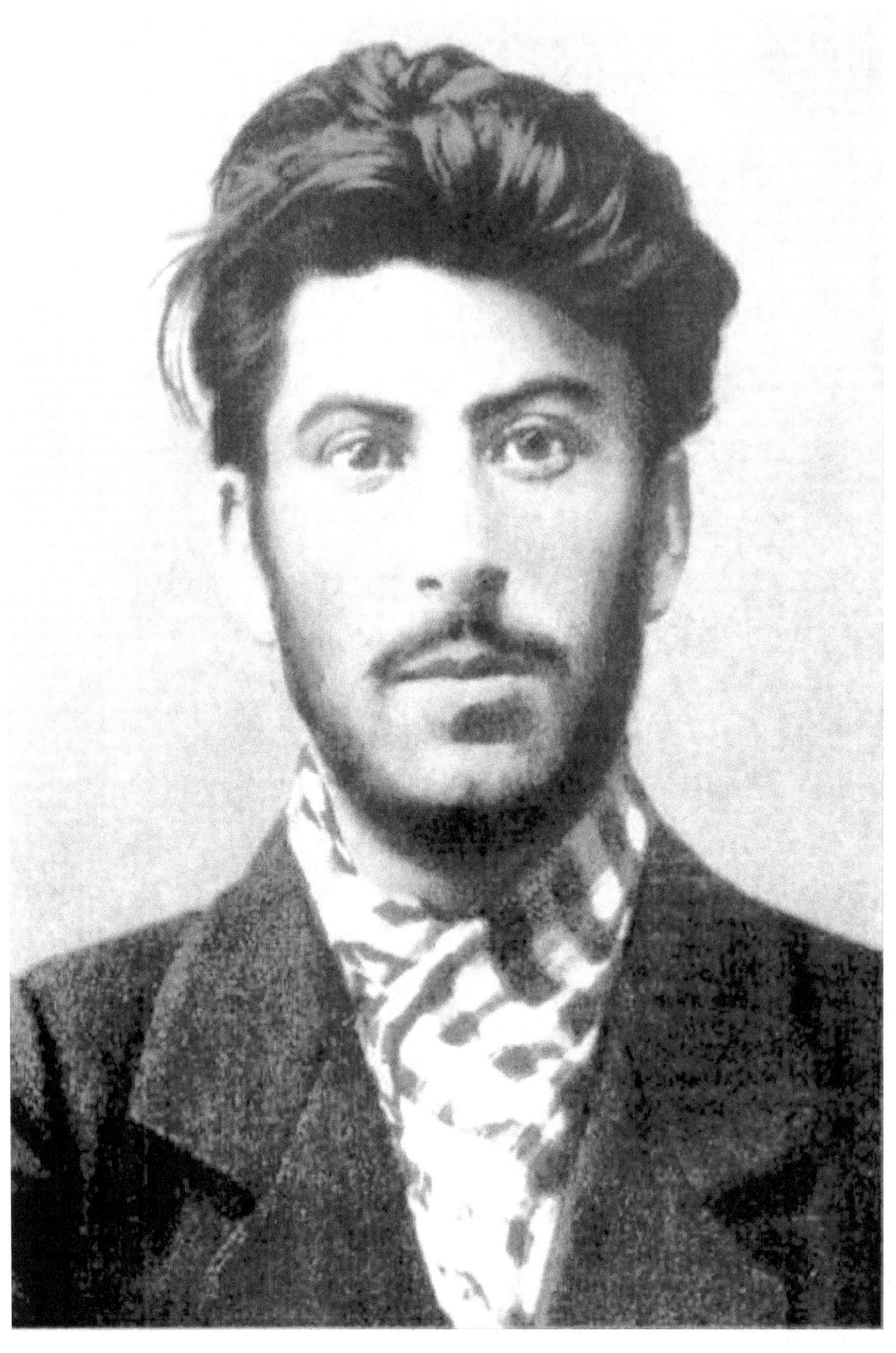

Stalin (23)

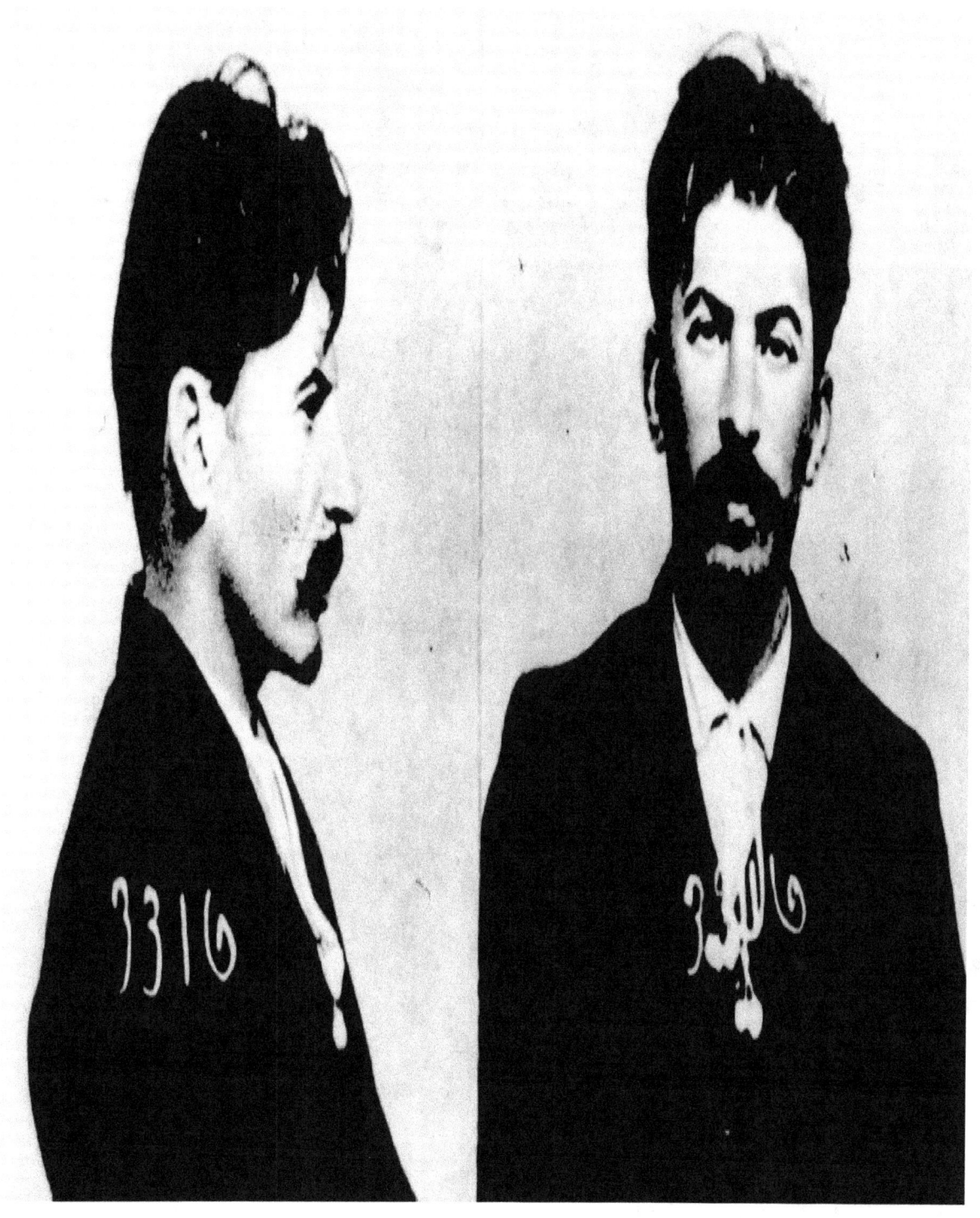

Prior to the revolution of 1917, Stalin played an active role in fighting the Russian government. Here he is shown on a 1911 information card from the files of the Russian police in Saint Petersburg.

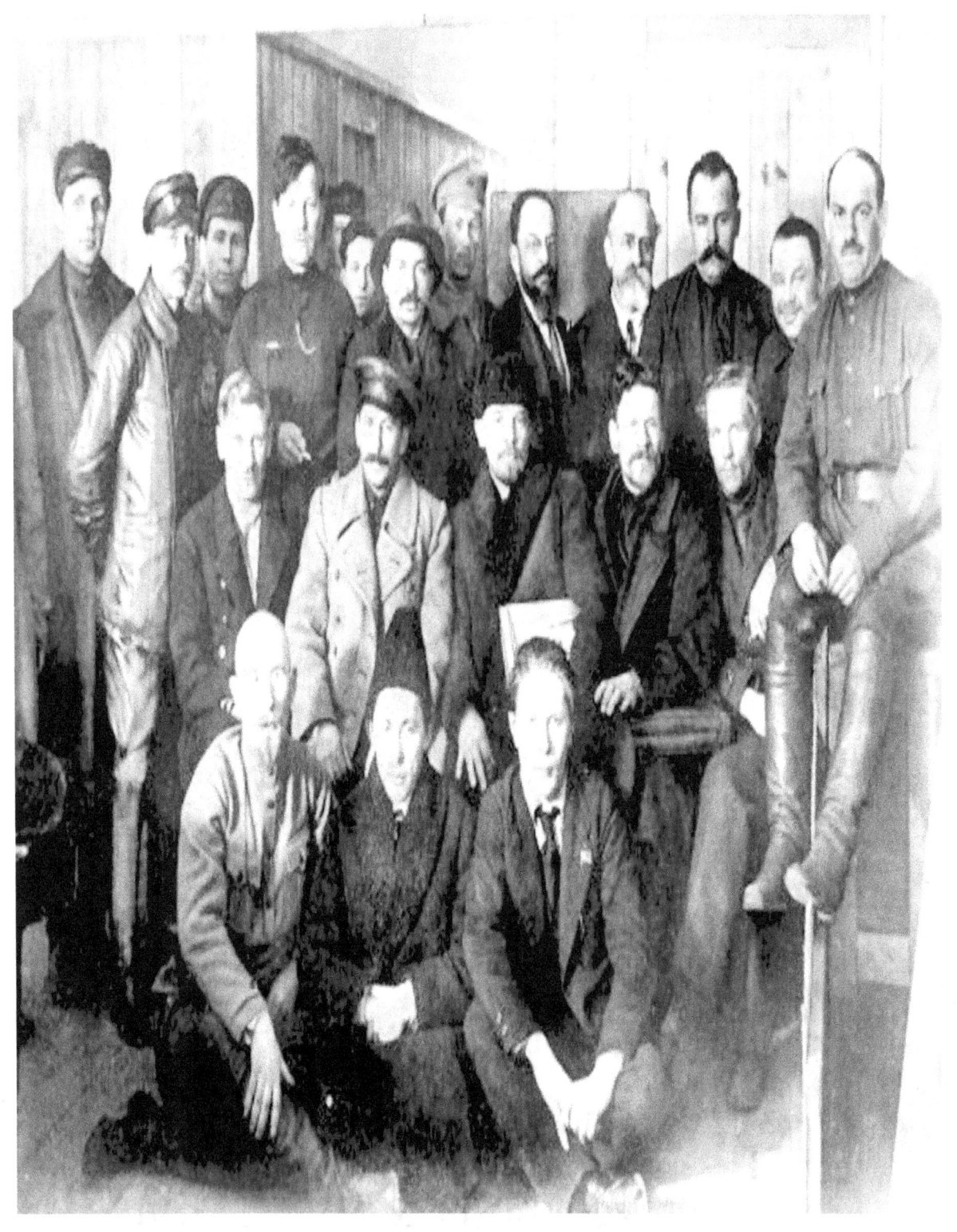

A group of participants in the 8th Congress of the Russian Communist Party, 1919. In the middle are Stalin, Vladimir Lenin, and Mikhail Kalinin.

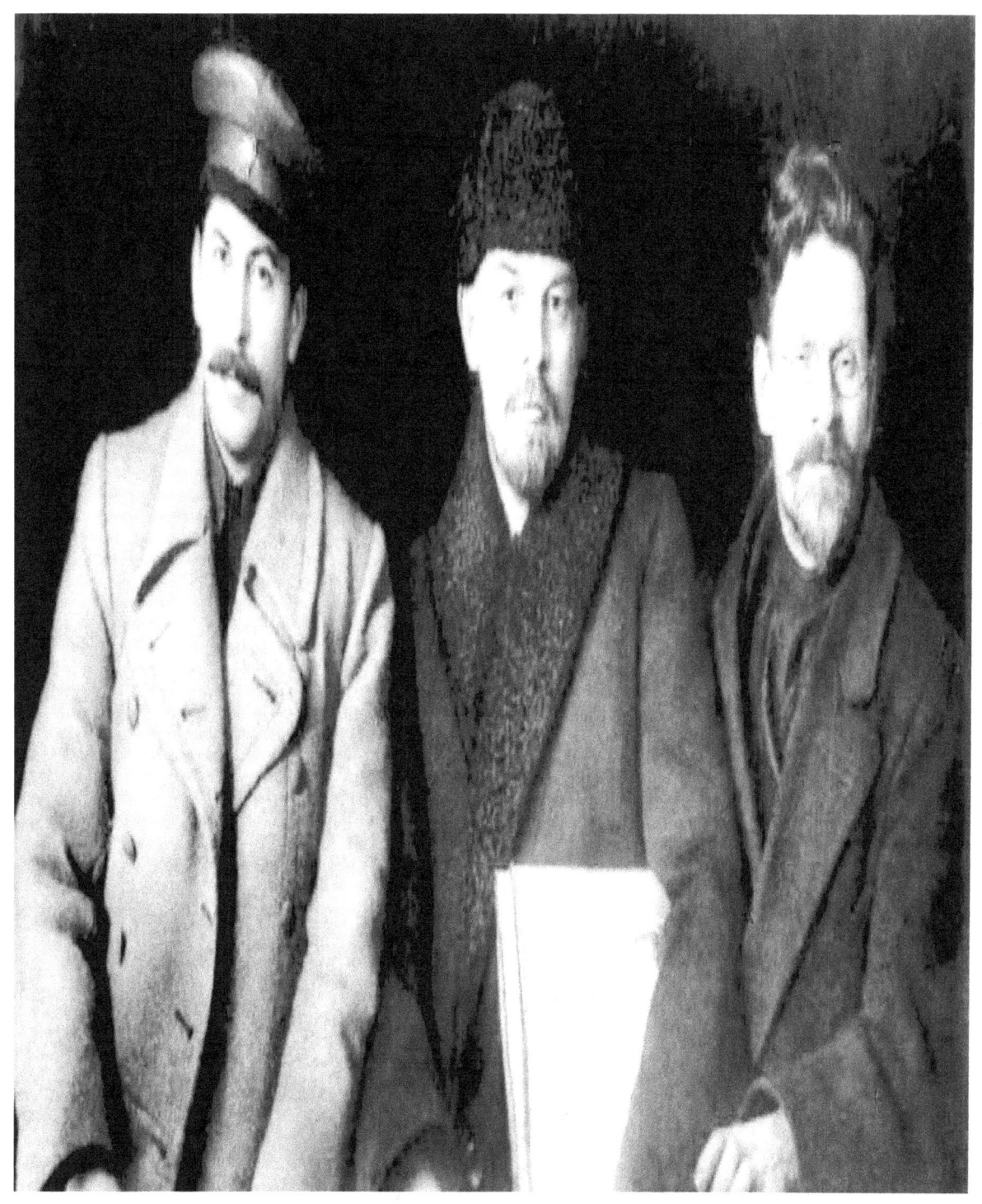

Joseph Stalin, Vladimir Lenin, and Mikhail Kalinin meeting in 1919. All three of them were "Old Bolsheviks" members of the Bolshevik party before the Russian Revolution of 1917.

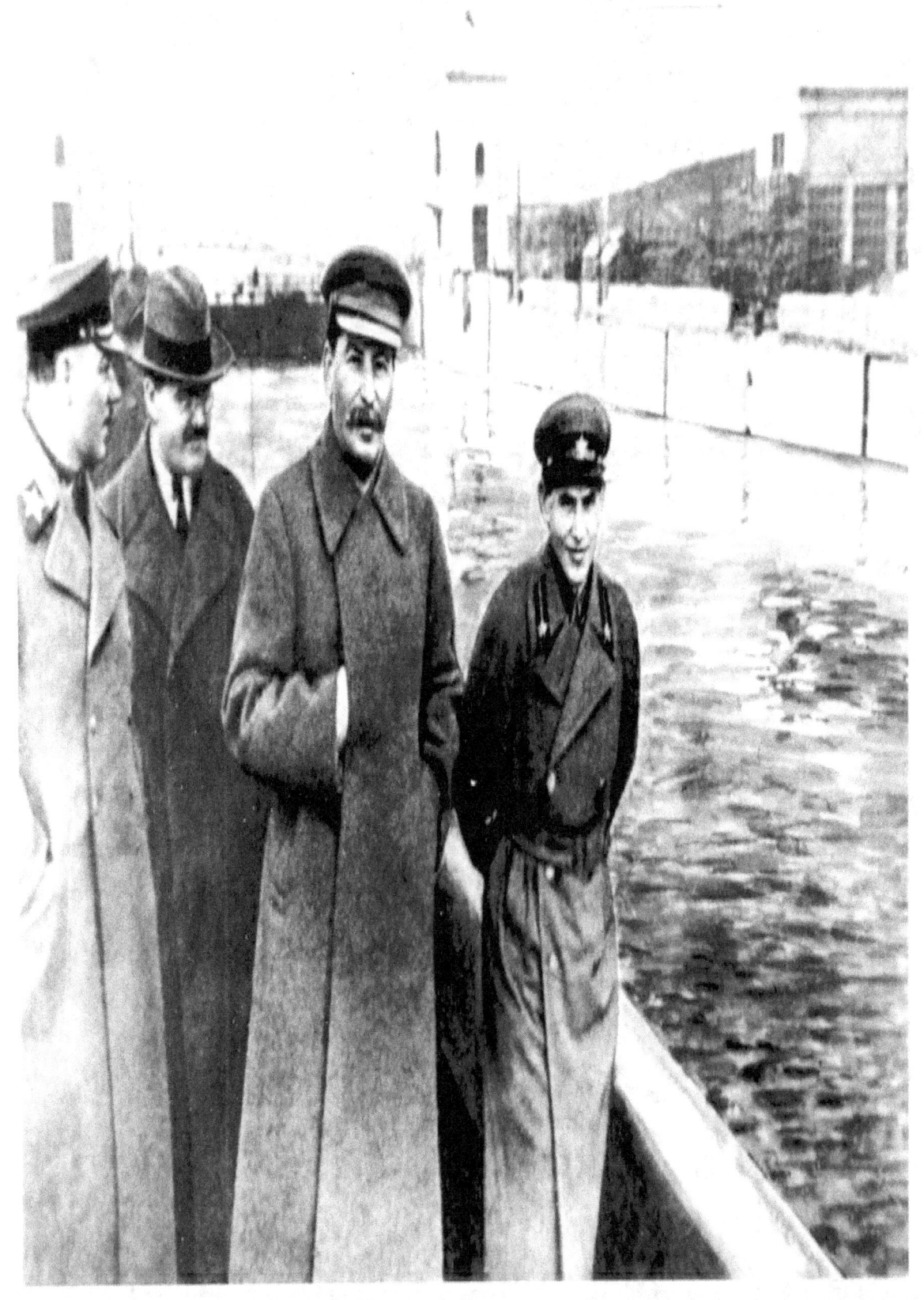

Nikolai Yezhov (right), walking with Stalin 1930s, was killed in 1940.

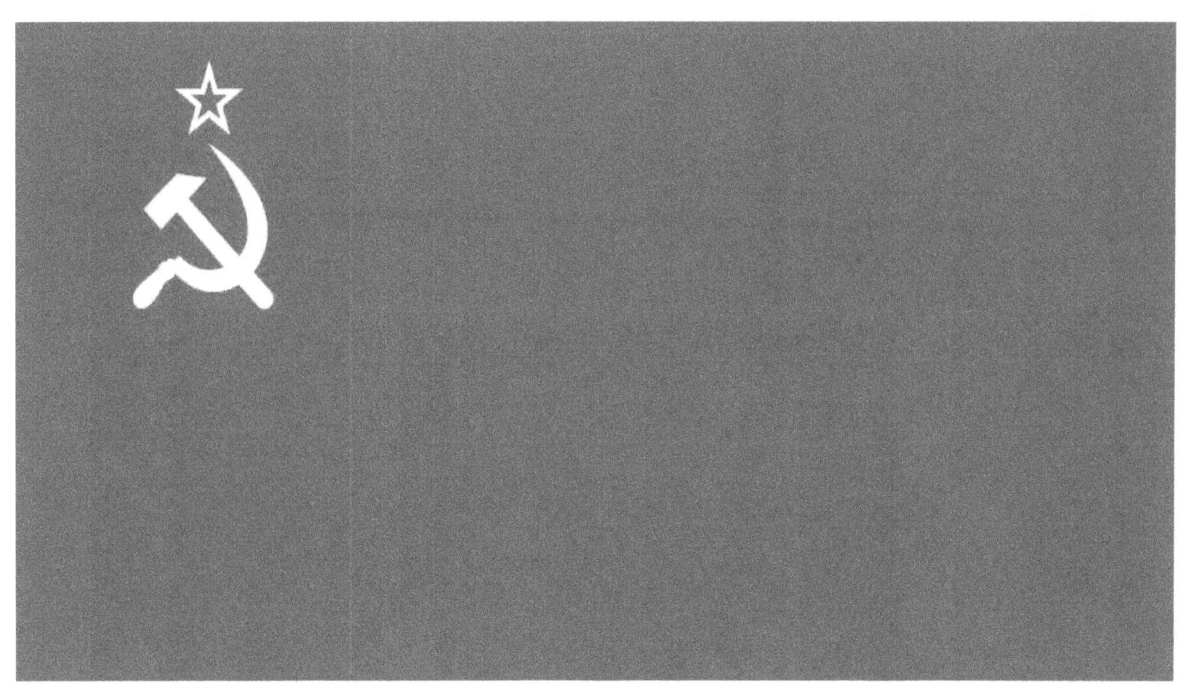

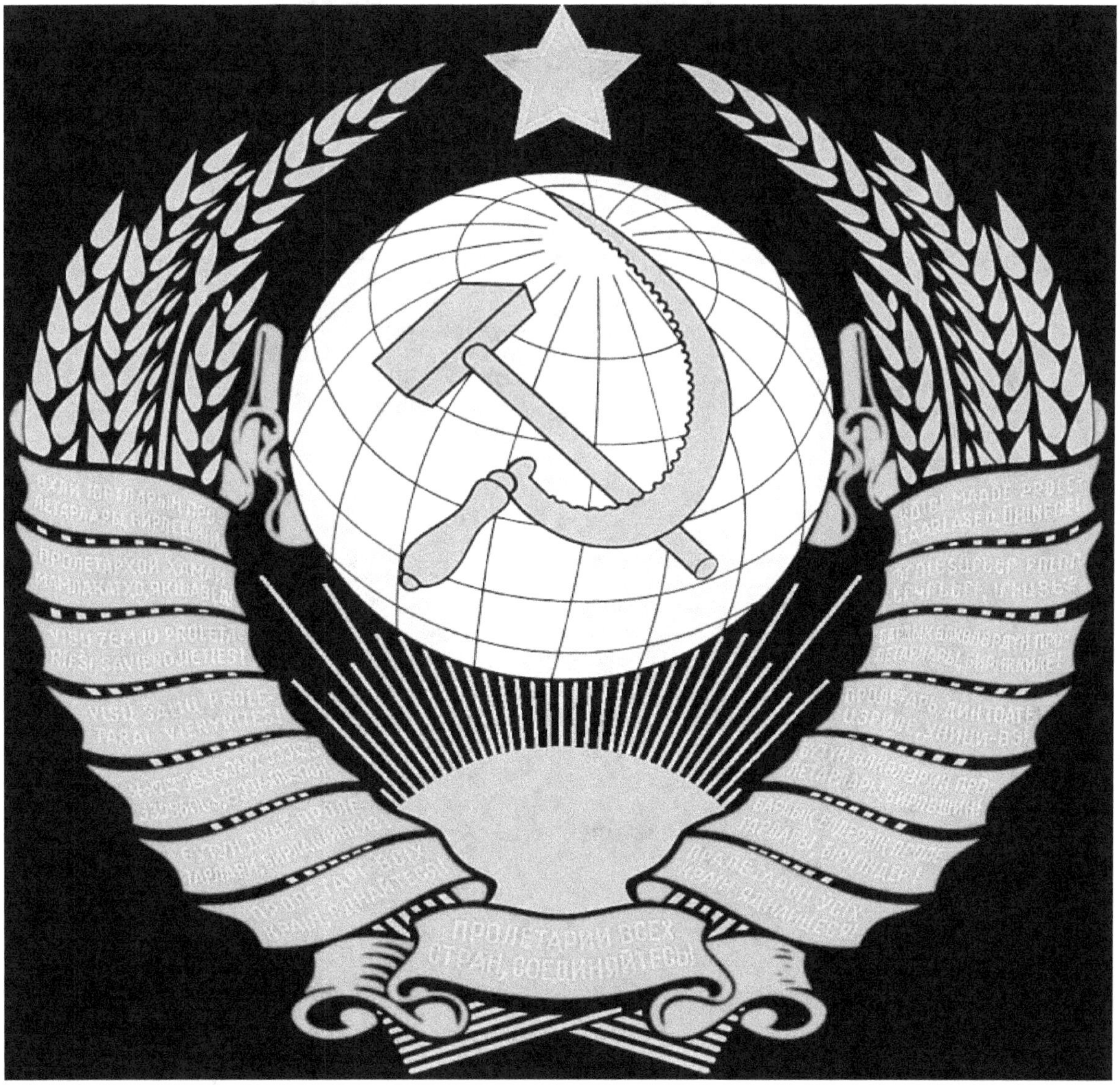

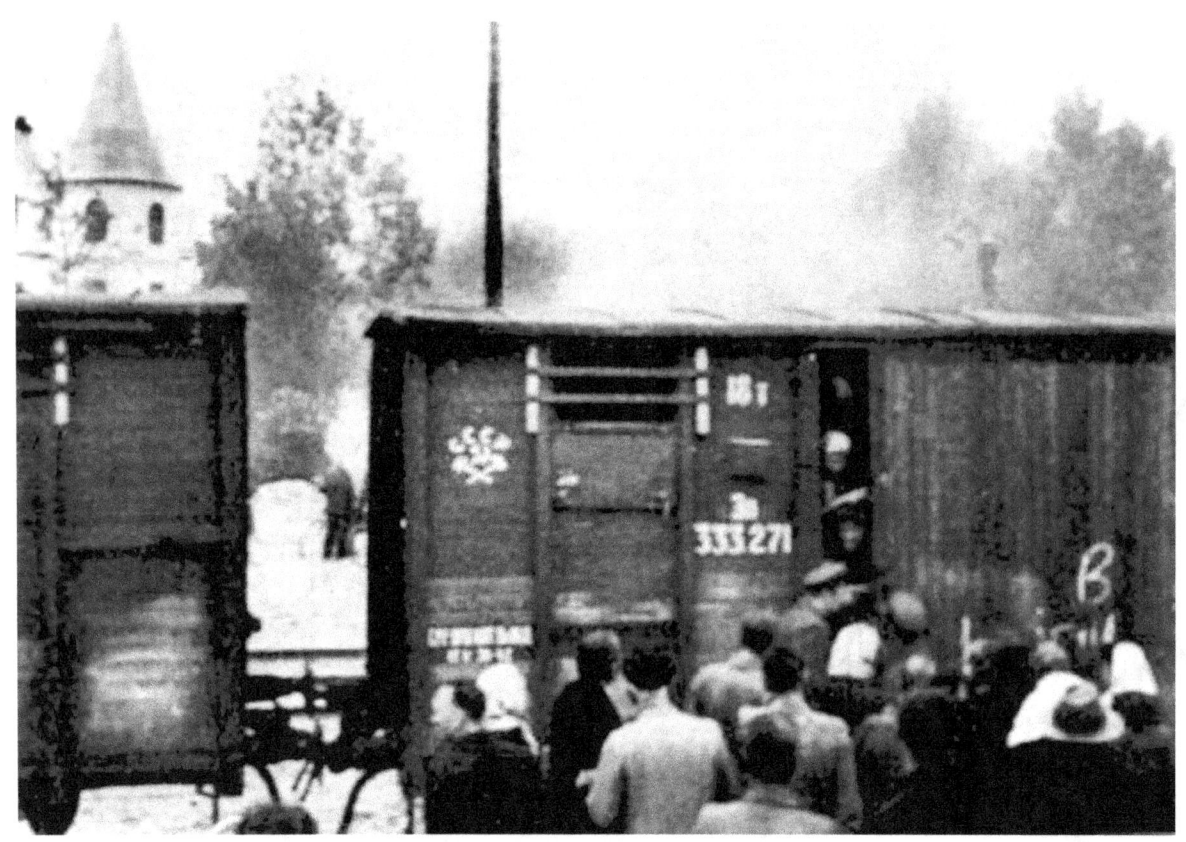

1941 <u>June deportation</u> in Latvia

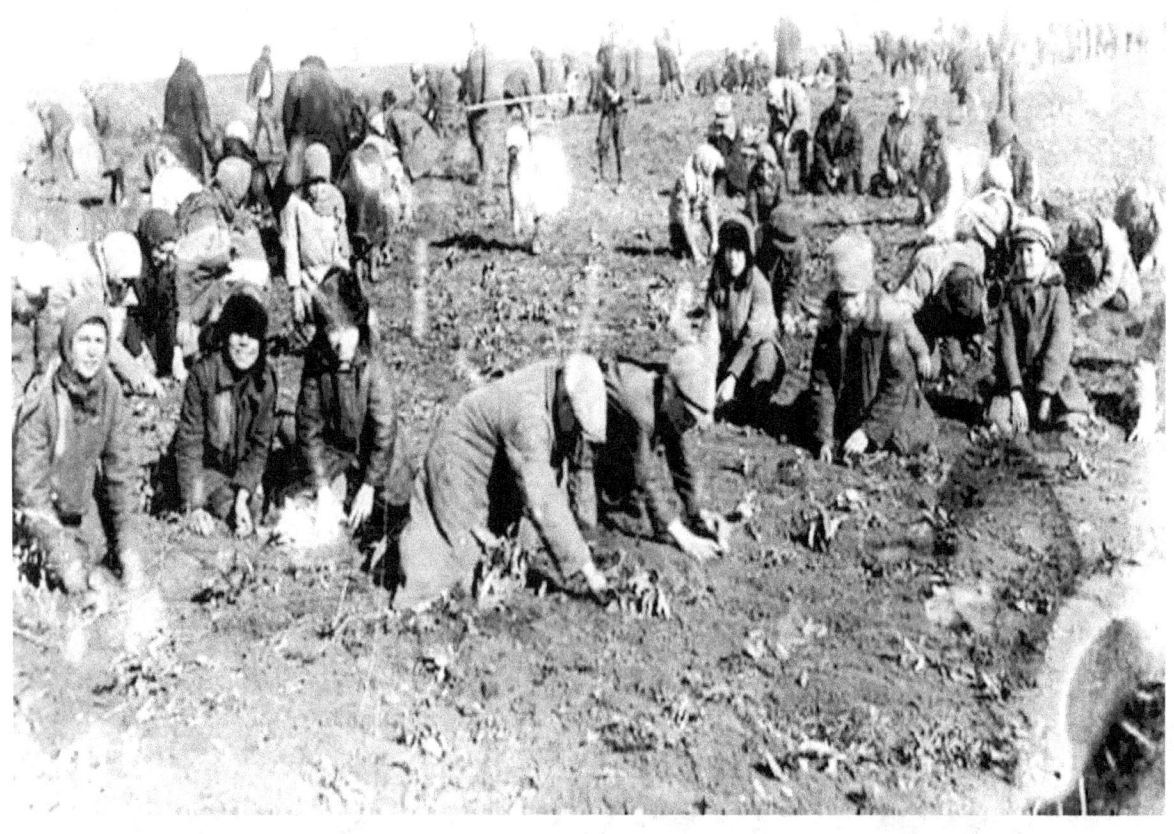

Children digging up frozen potatoes in the field of a collective farm, 1933

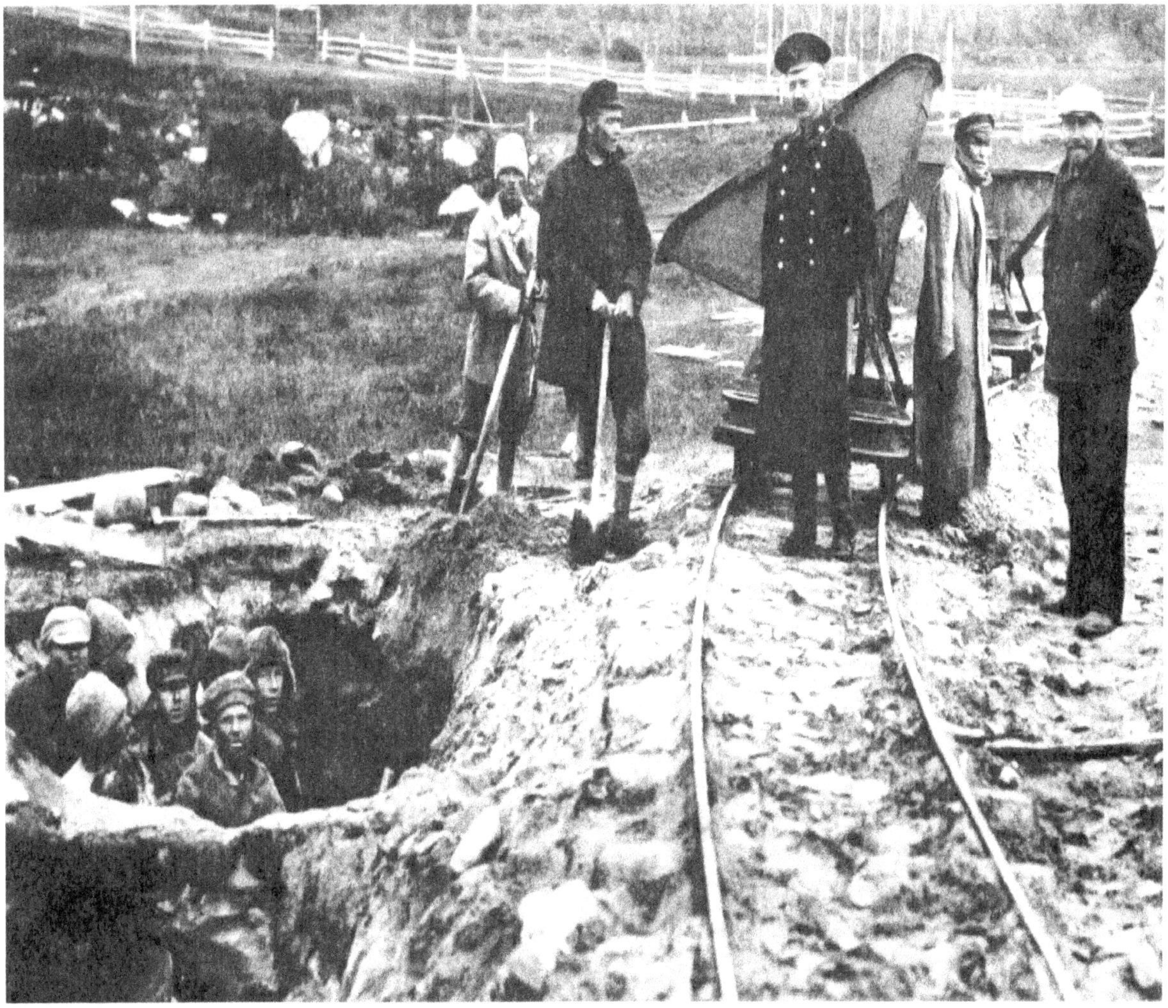

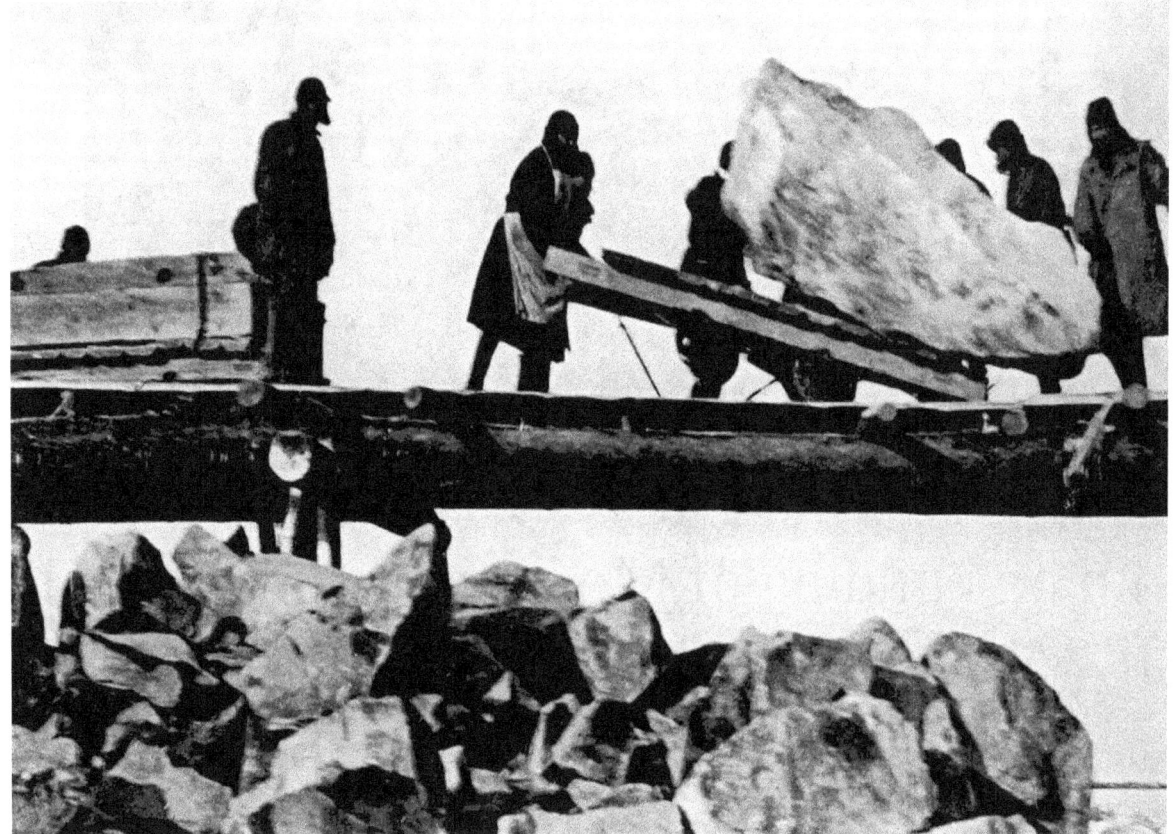

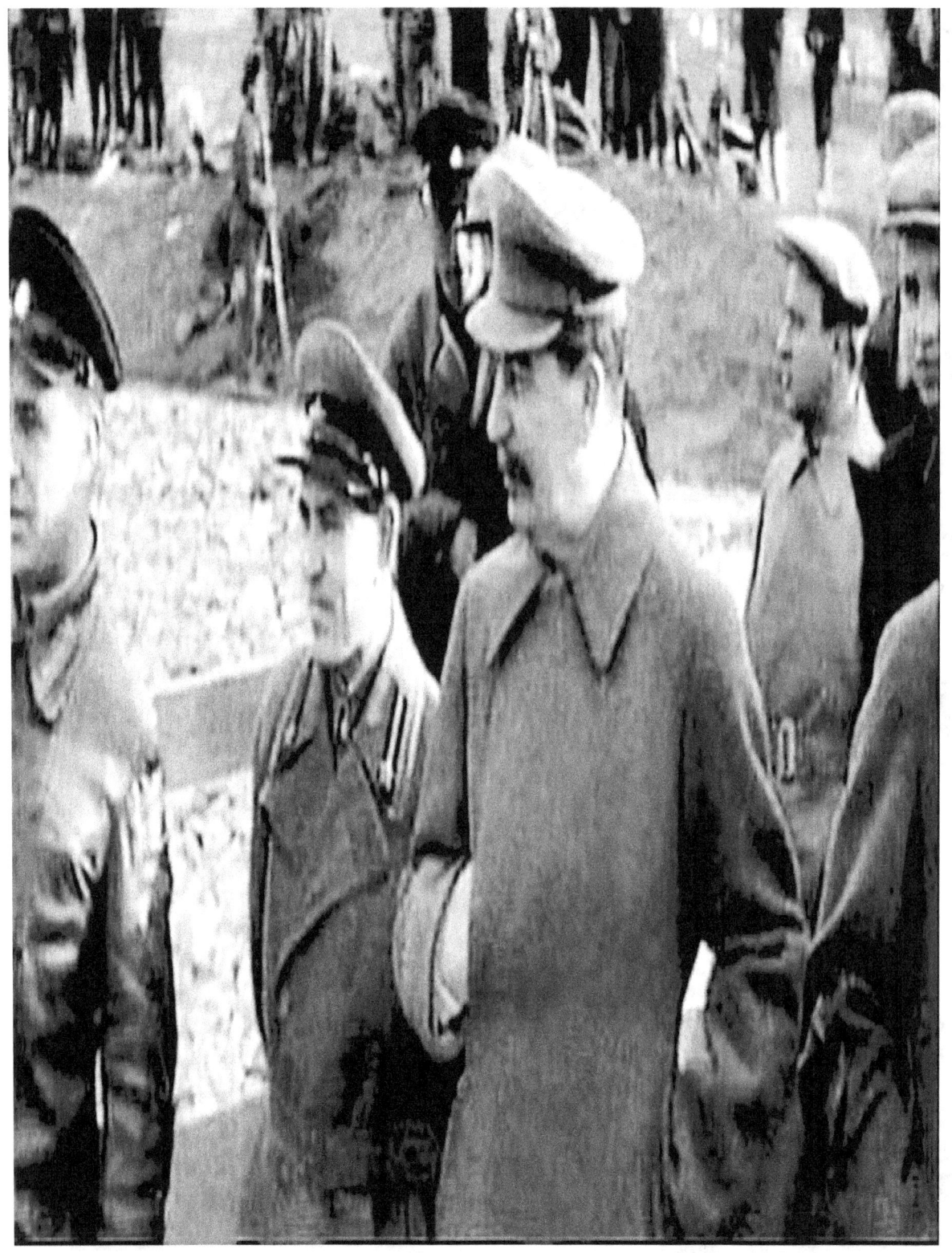

Stalin on building of <u>Moscow-Volga canal</u>.
It was constructed from 1932 to 1937
by <u>Gulag</u> prisoners.

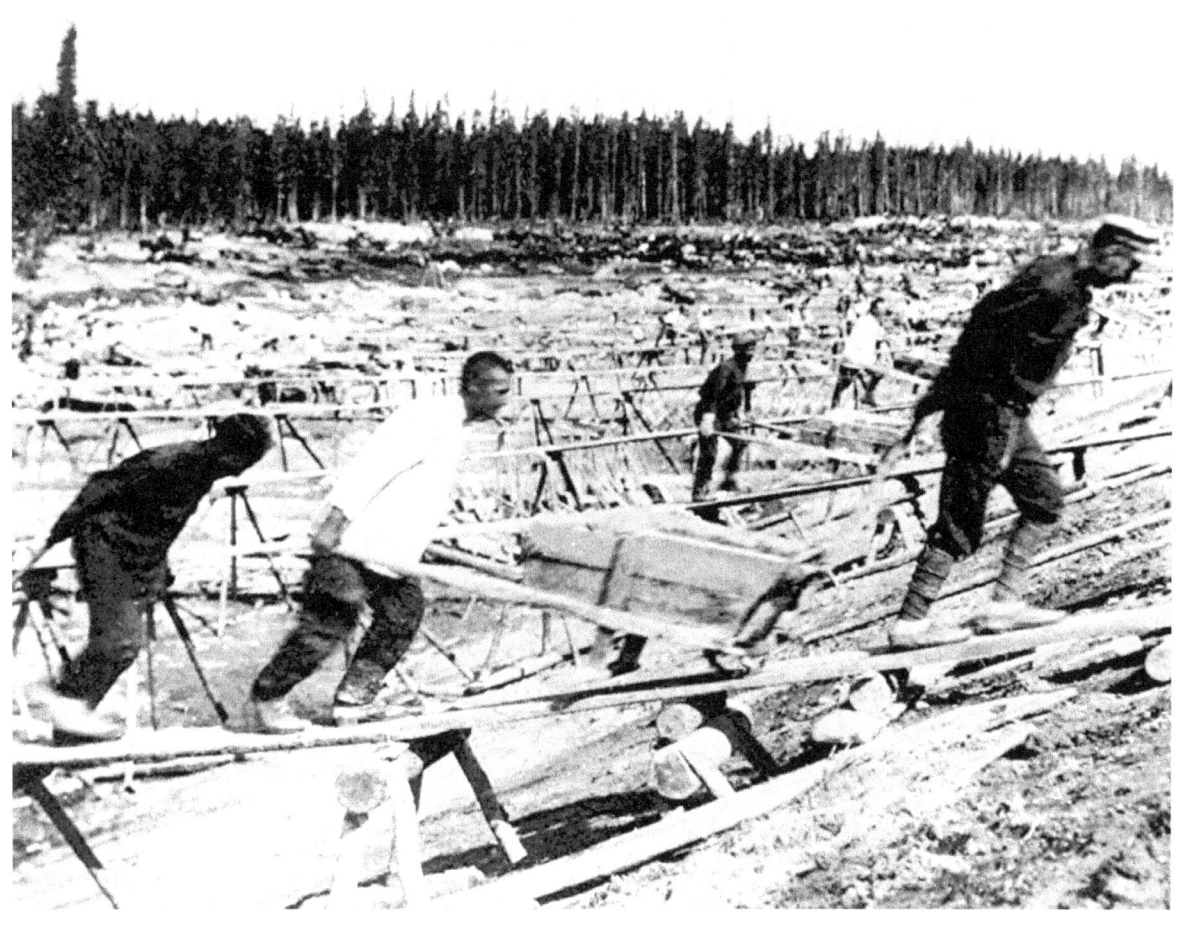

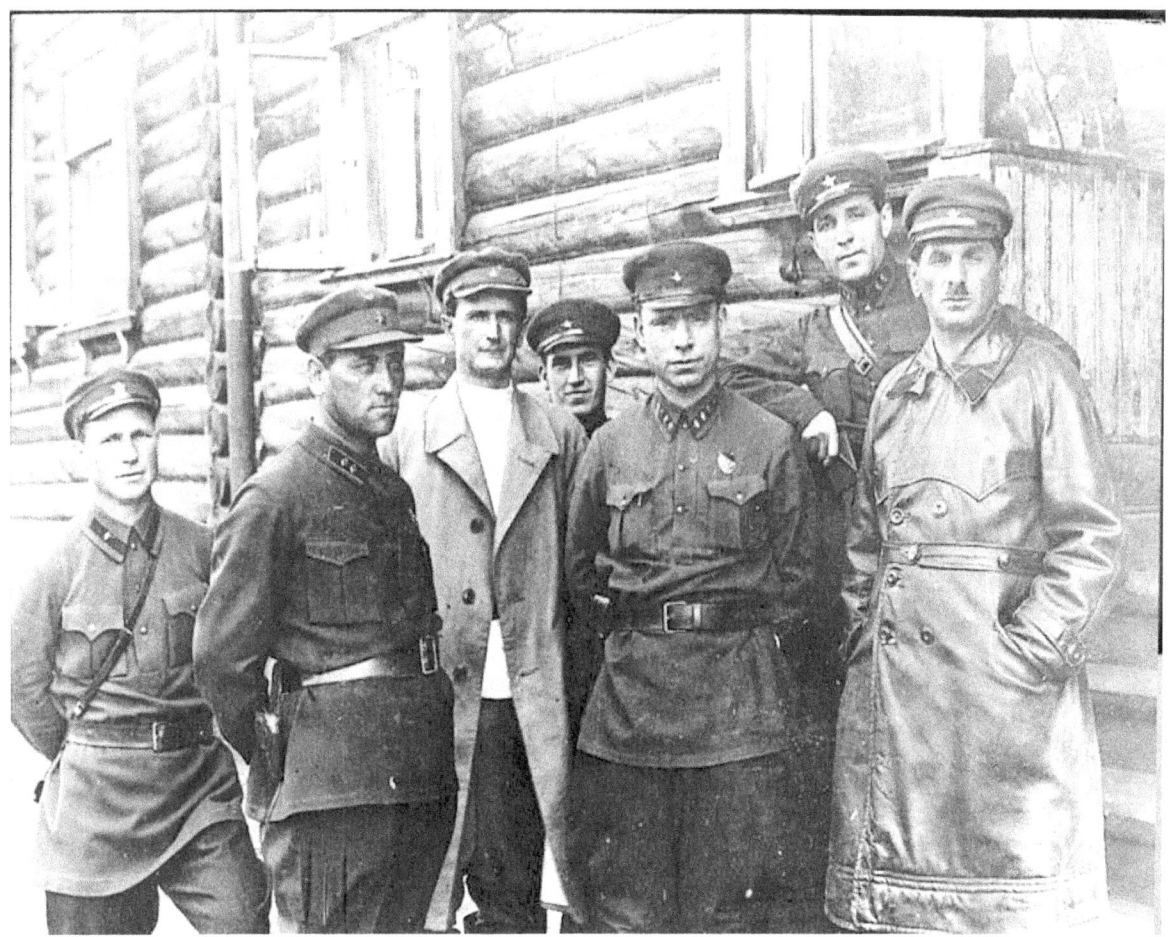

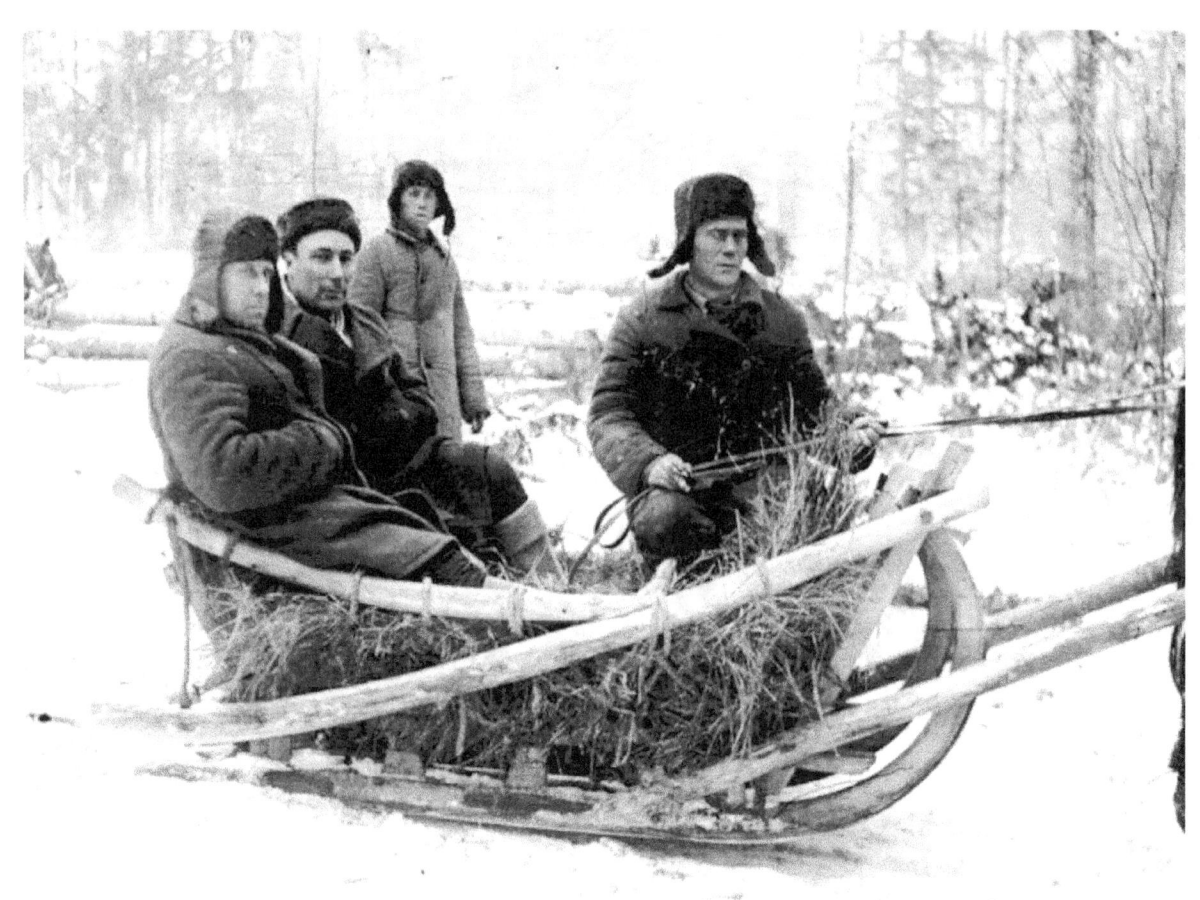

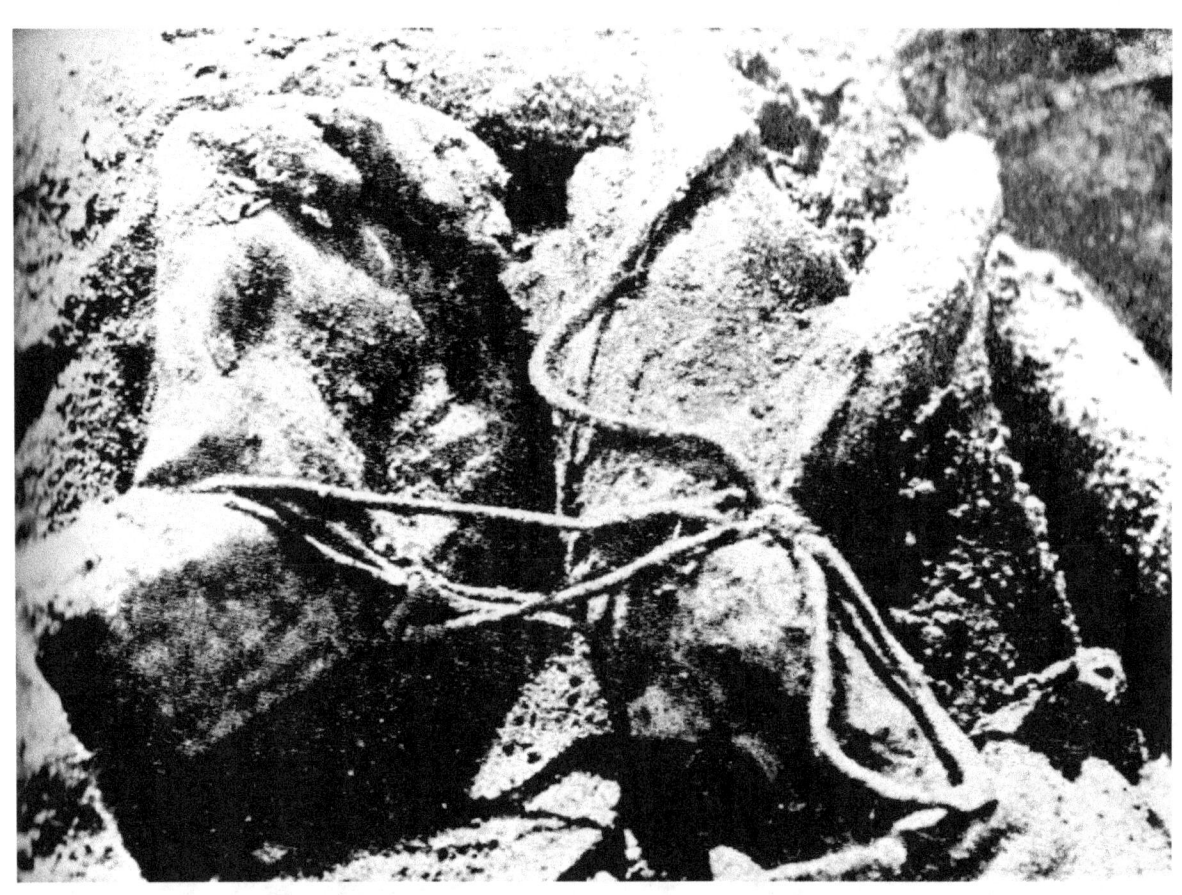

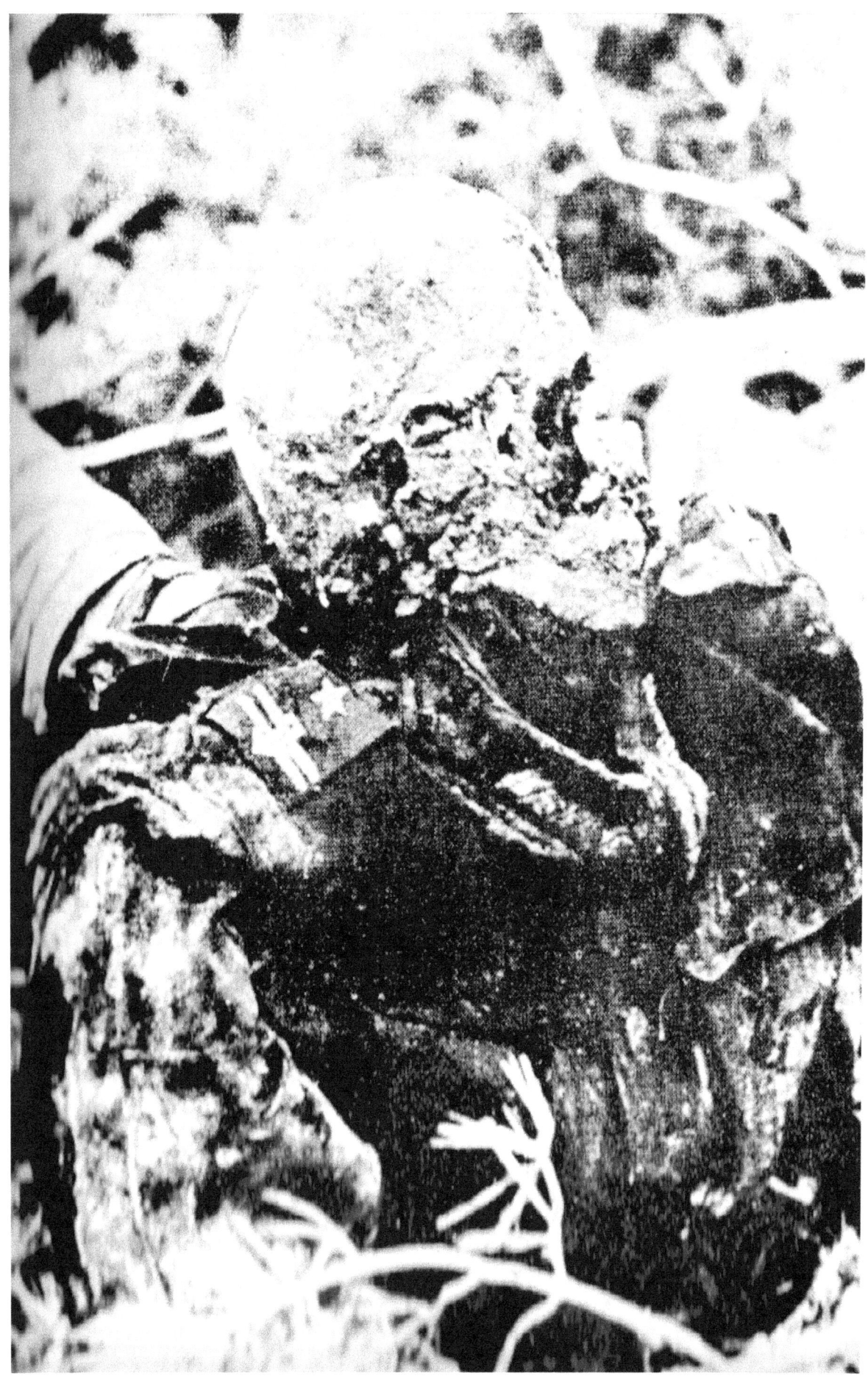

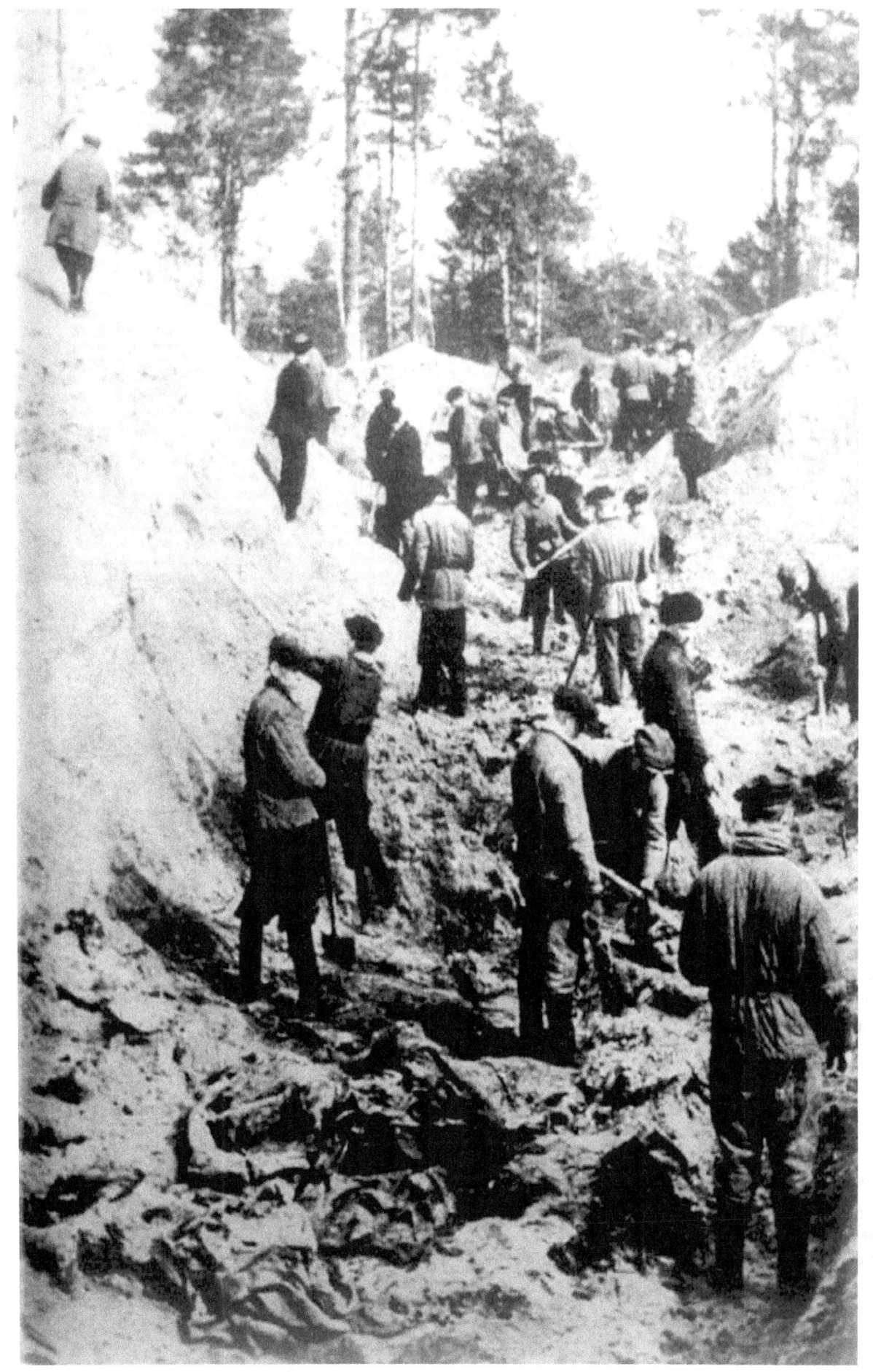

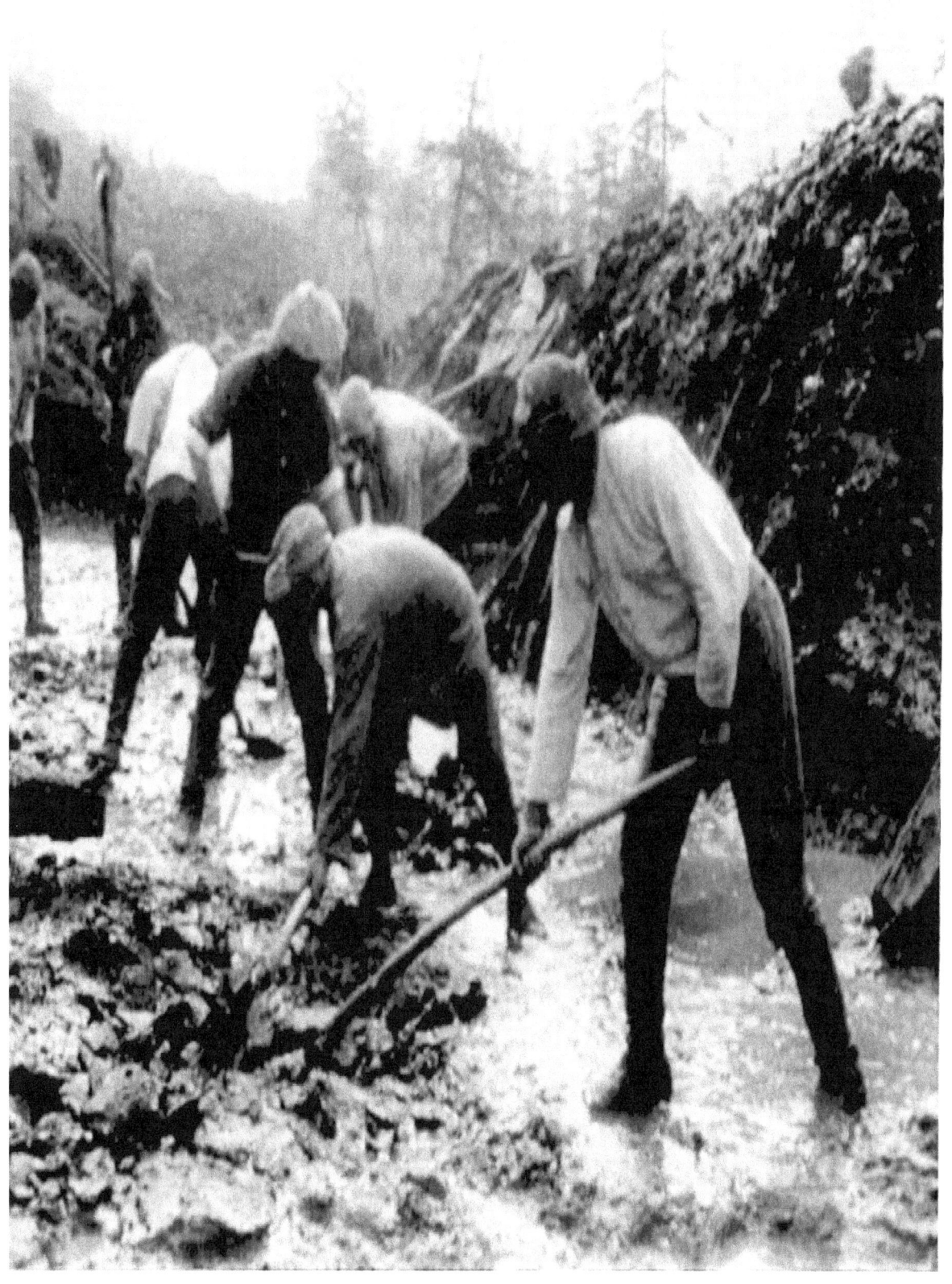

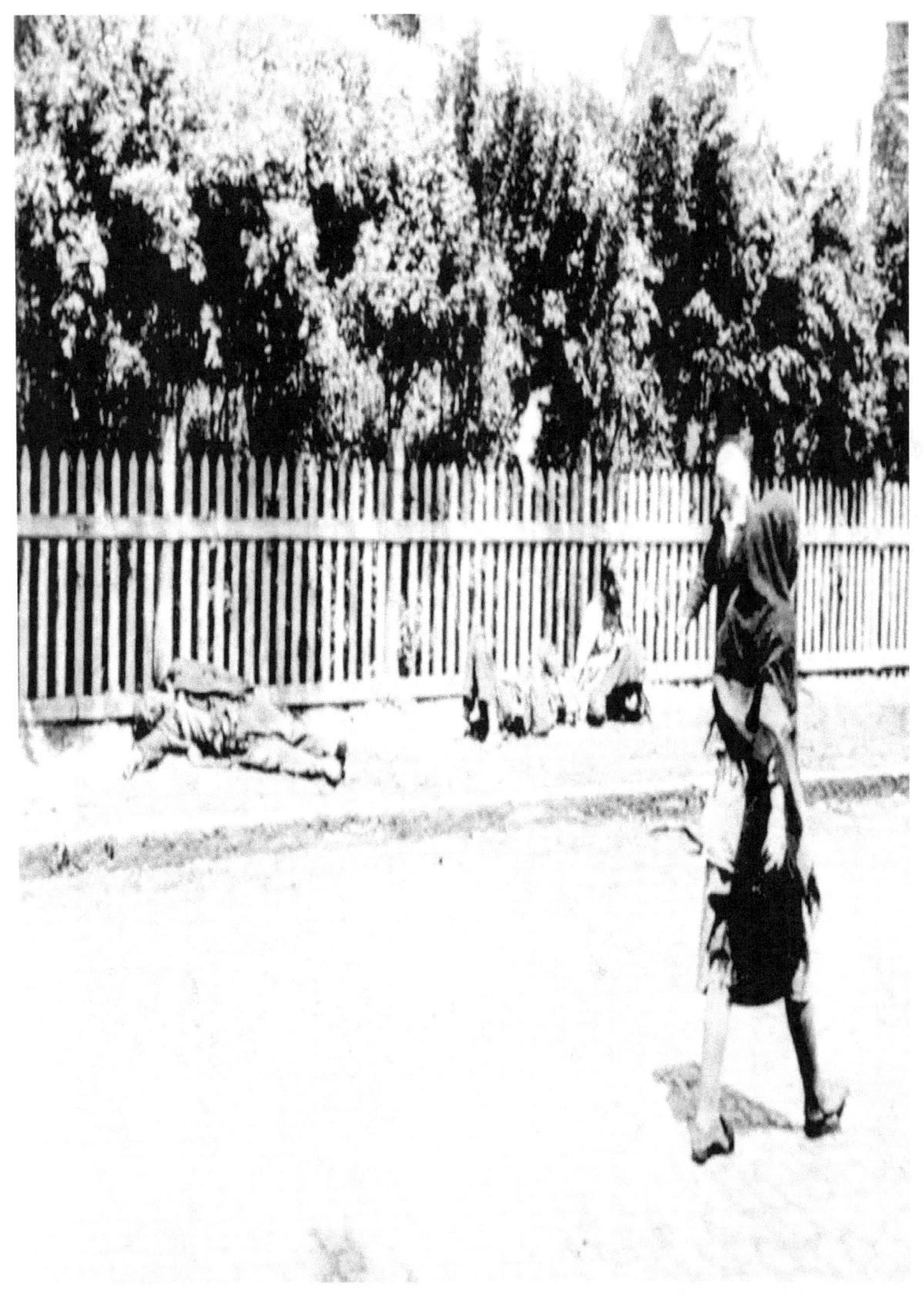

Starved peasants on a street in <u>Kharkiv</u>, 1933.

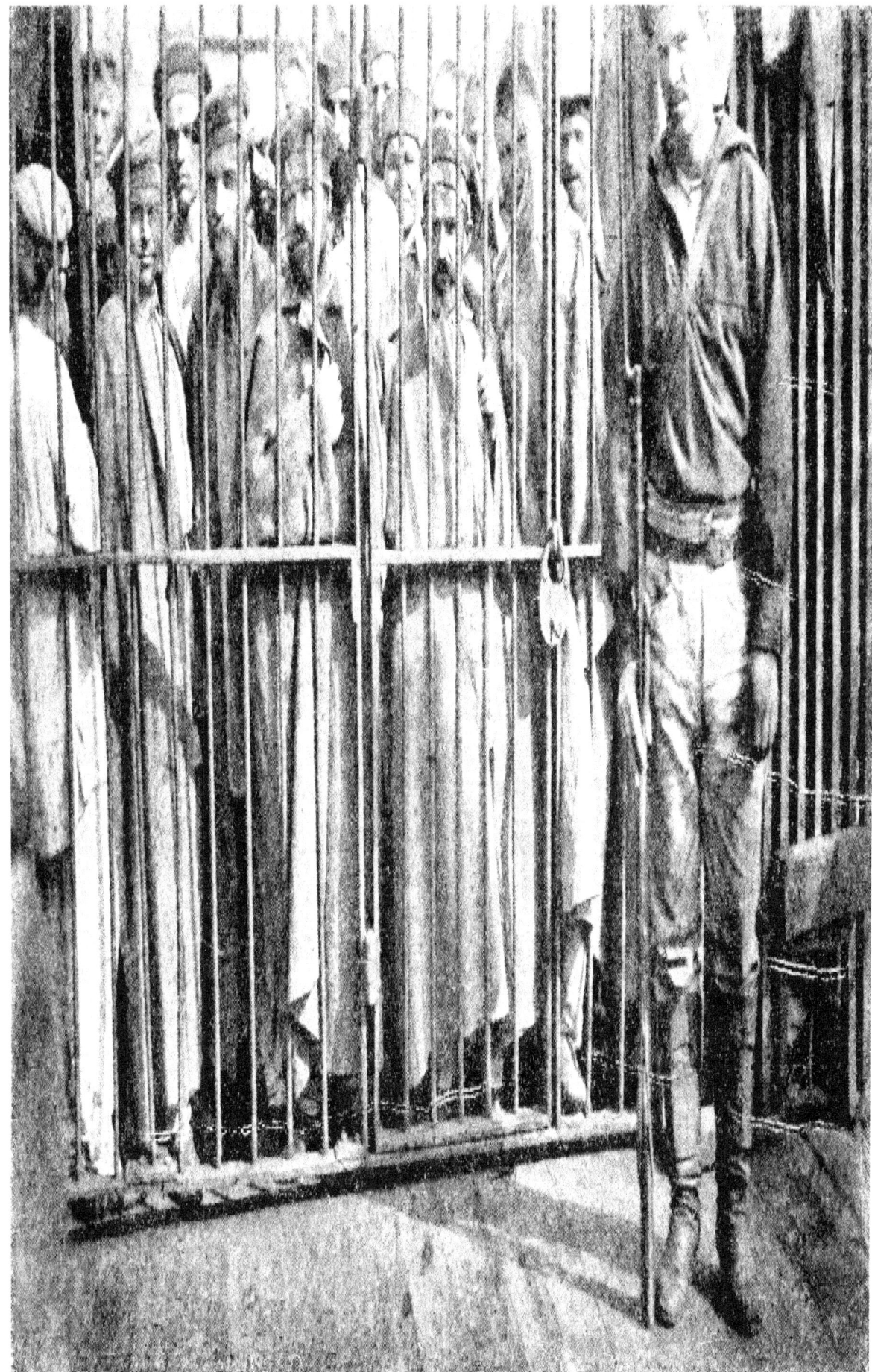

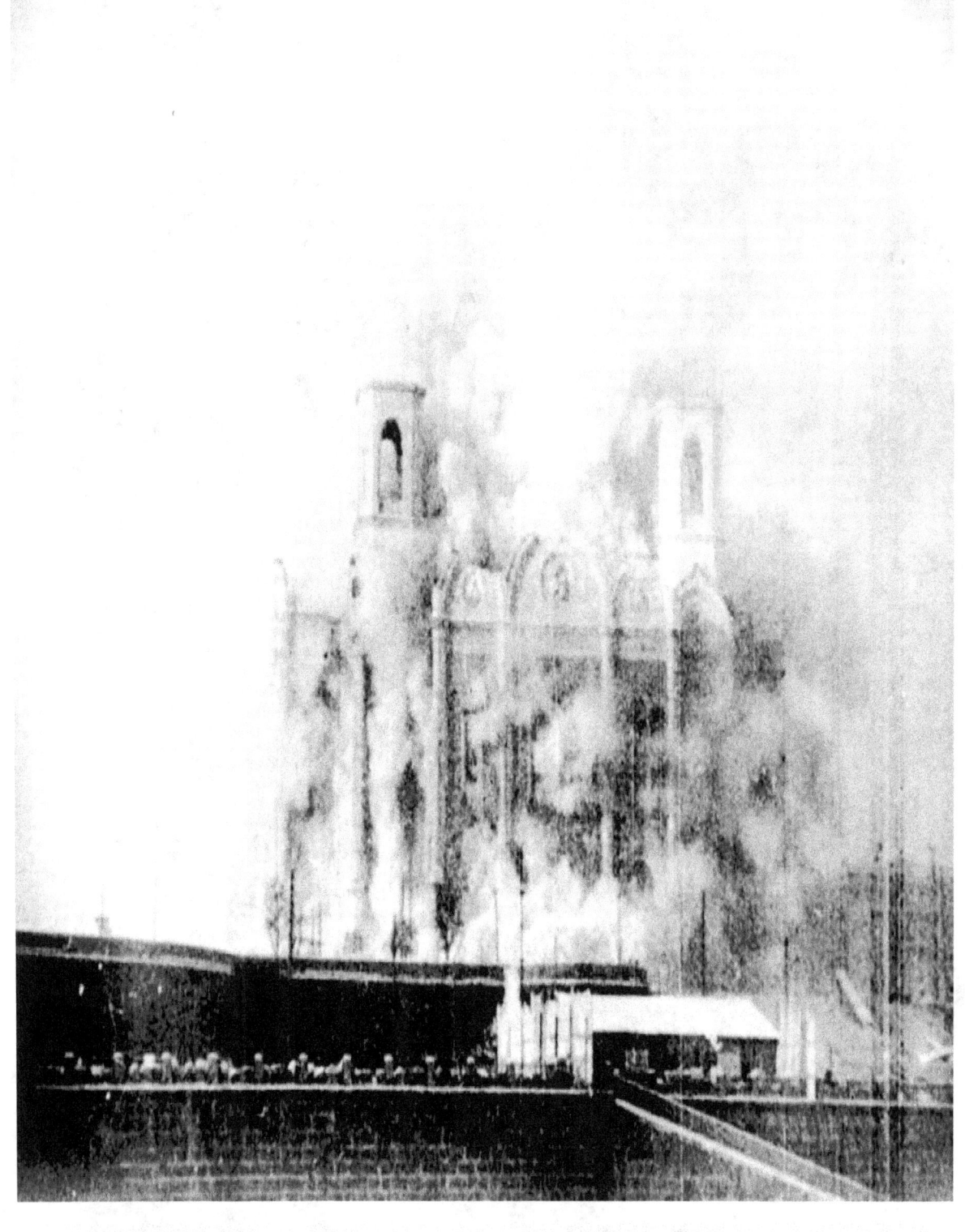

Photograph taken of the 1931 demolition
of the <u>Cathedral of Christ the Saviour</u> in
Moscow.

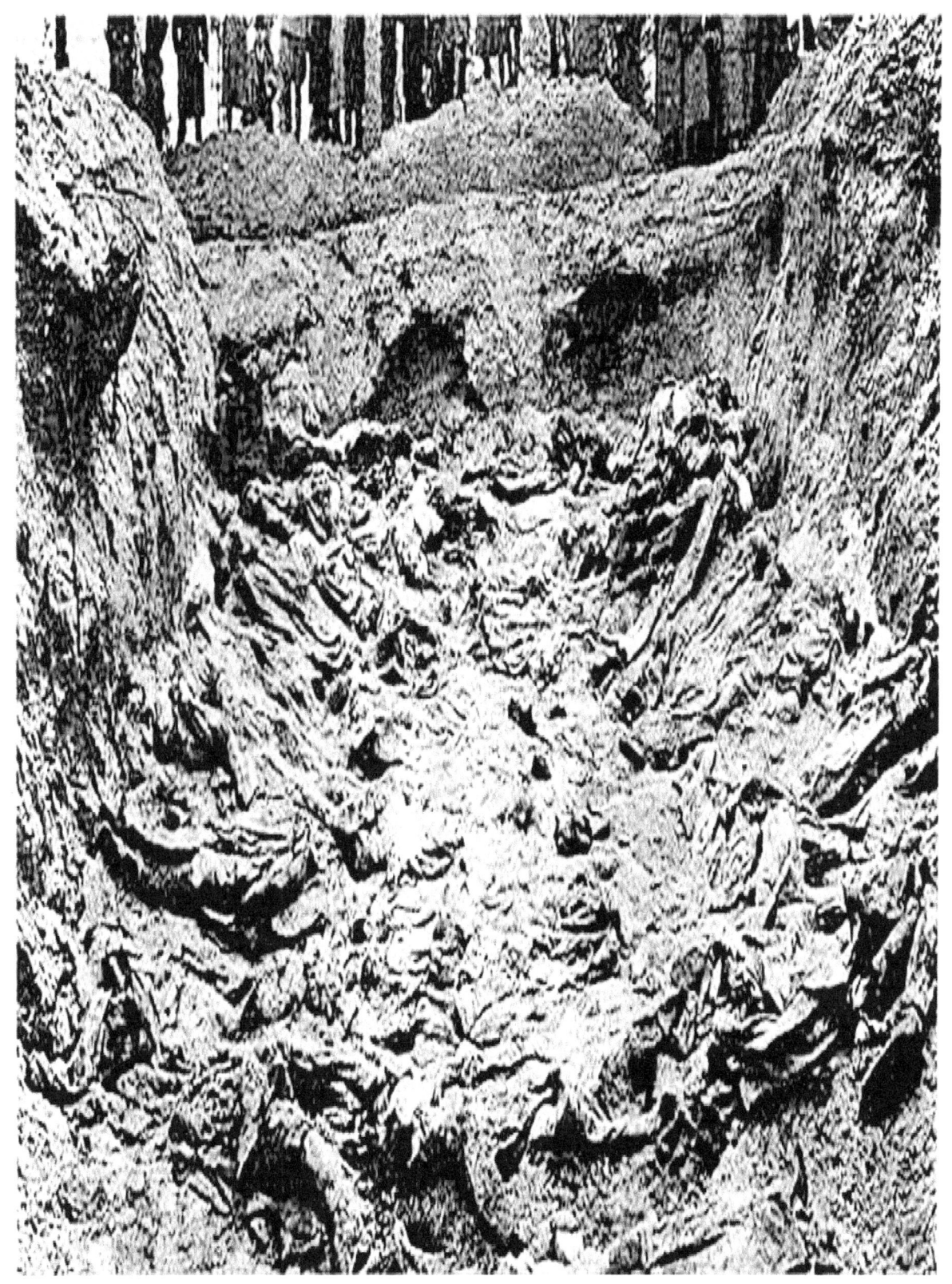

Photo from 1943 exhumation of mass grave of Polish officers killed by NKVD in Katyń Forest in 1940.

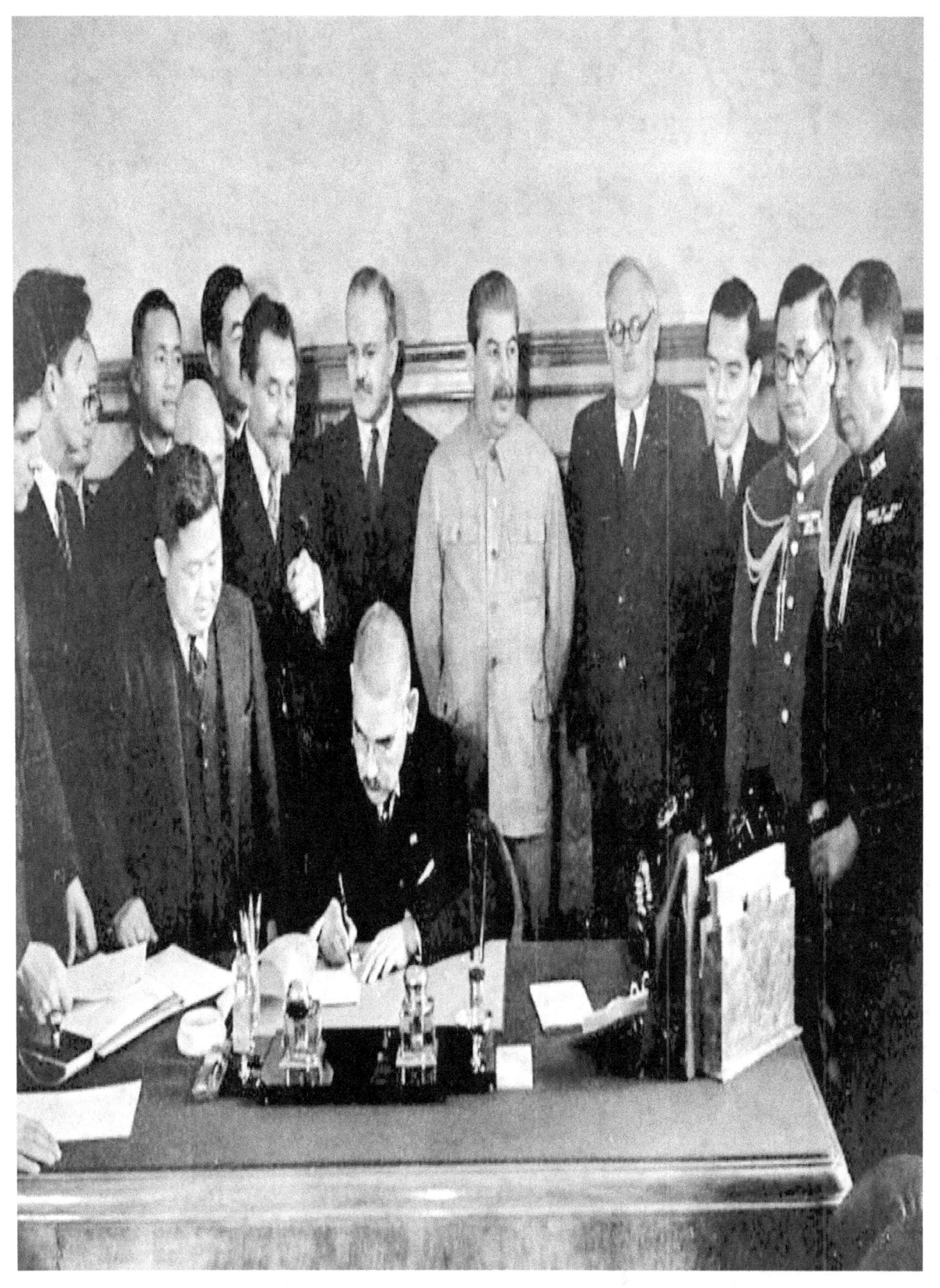

Stalin and Molotov at the signing of
the <u>Soviet–Japanese Neutrality Pact</u> with
the <u>Empire of Japan</u>, 1941

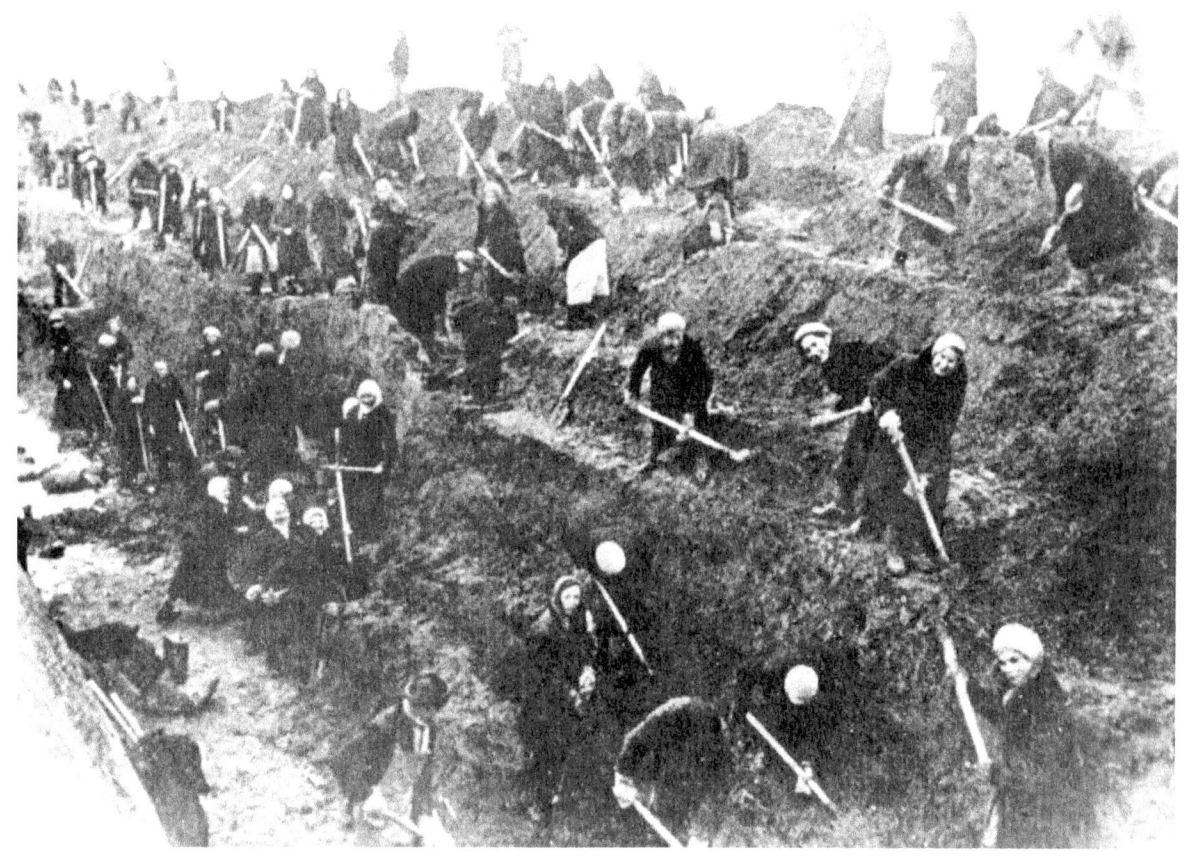

With all the men at the front, Moscow women dig <u>anti-tank trenches</u>around Moscow in 1941.

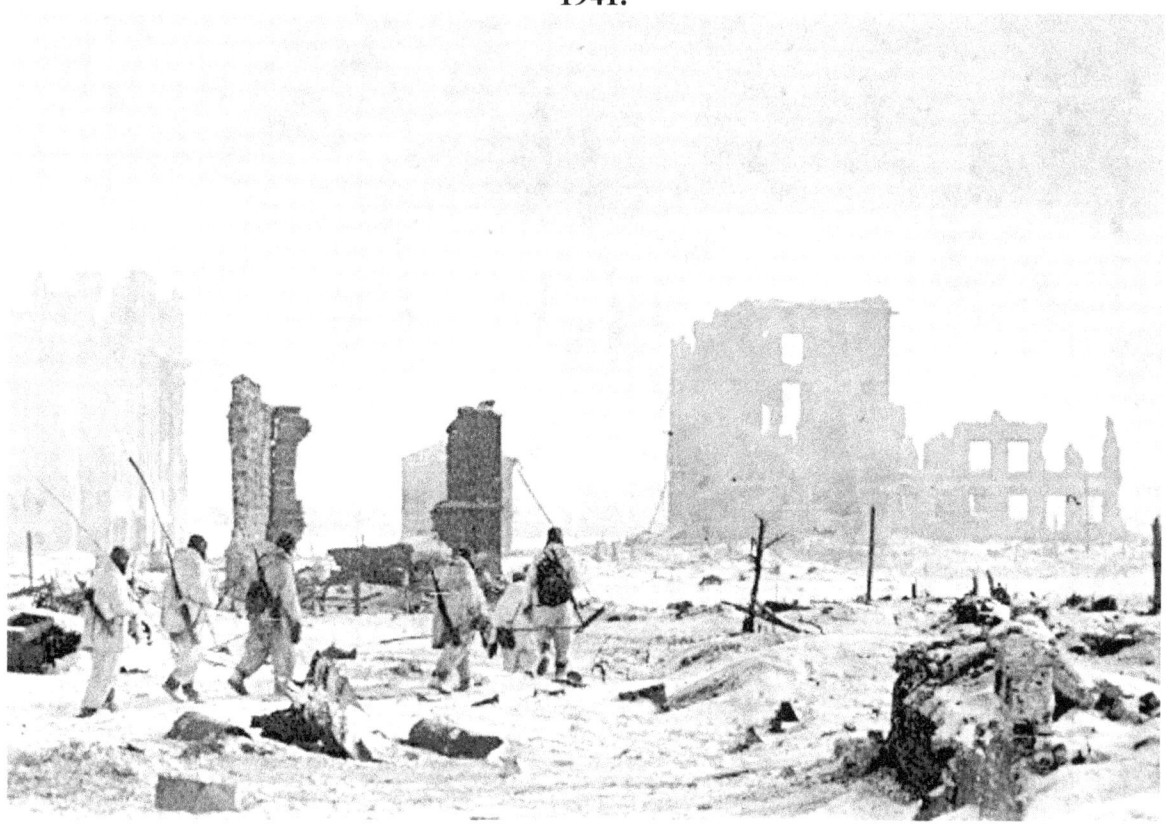

The center of <u>Stalingrad</u> after liberation, 2 February 1943.

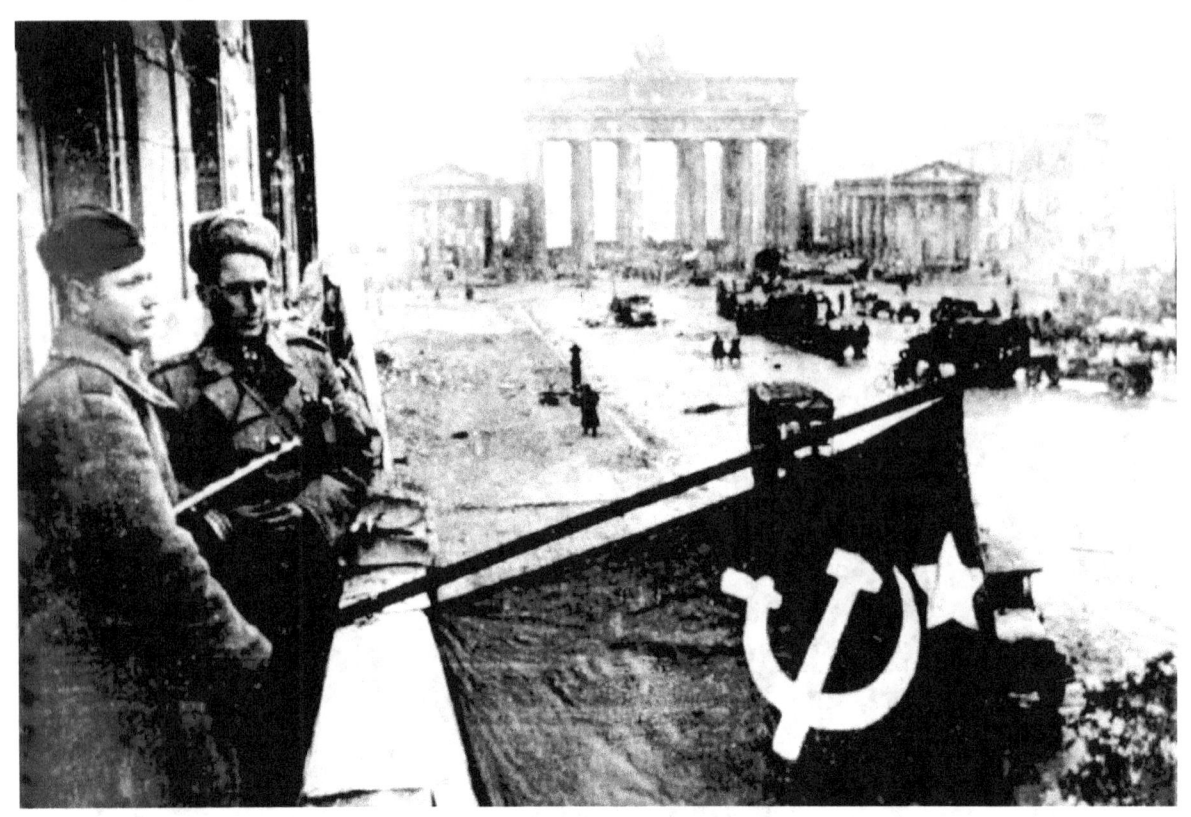

Victorious Soviet soldiers in Berlin, 1945.

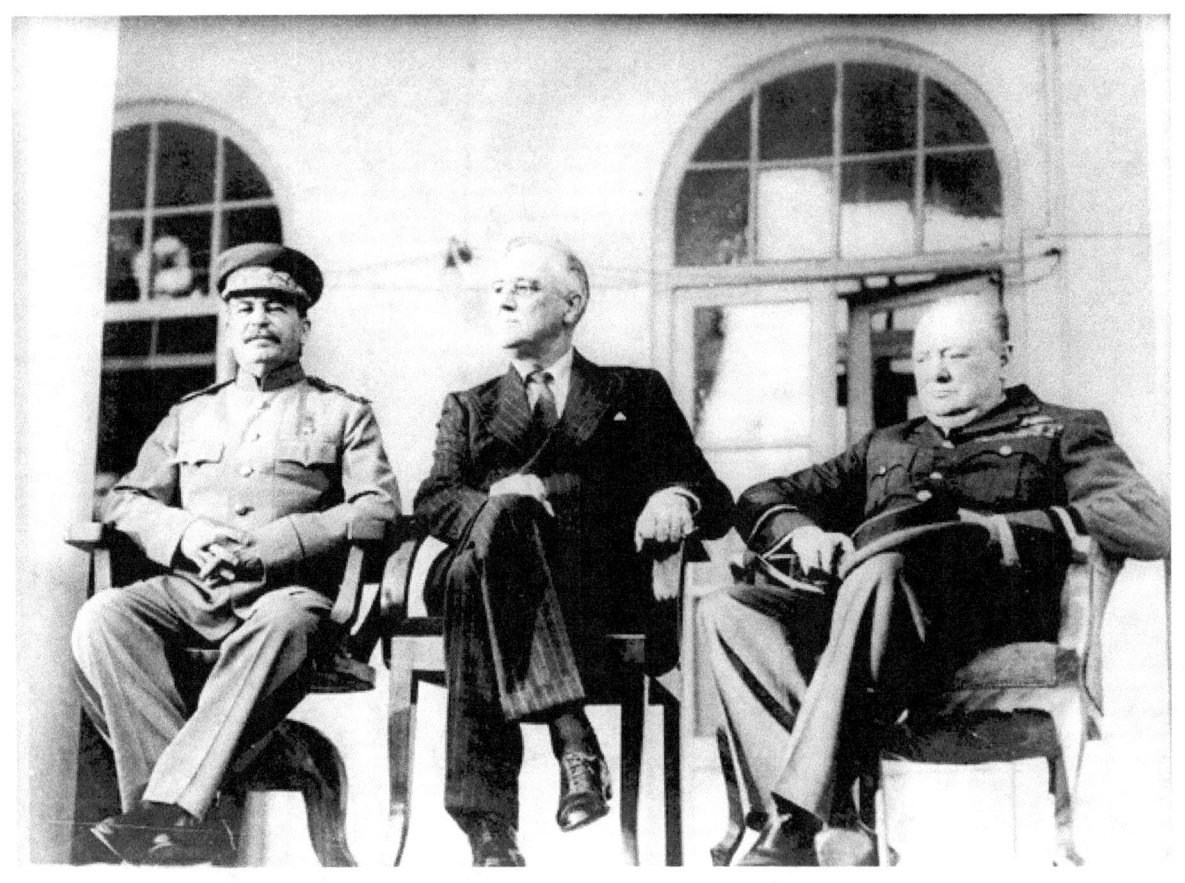

The Big Three: Stalin, <u>U.S. President</u> <u>Franklin D. Roosevelt</u>, and <u>British Prime Minister</u> <u>Winston Churchill</u> at the <u>Tehran Conference</u>, November 1943.

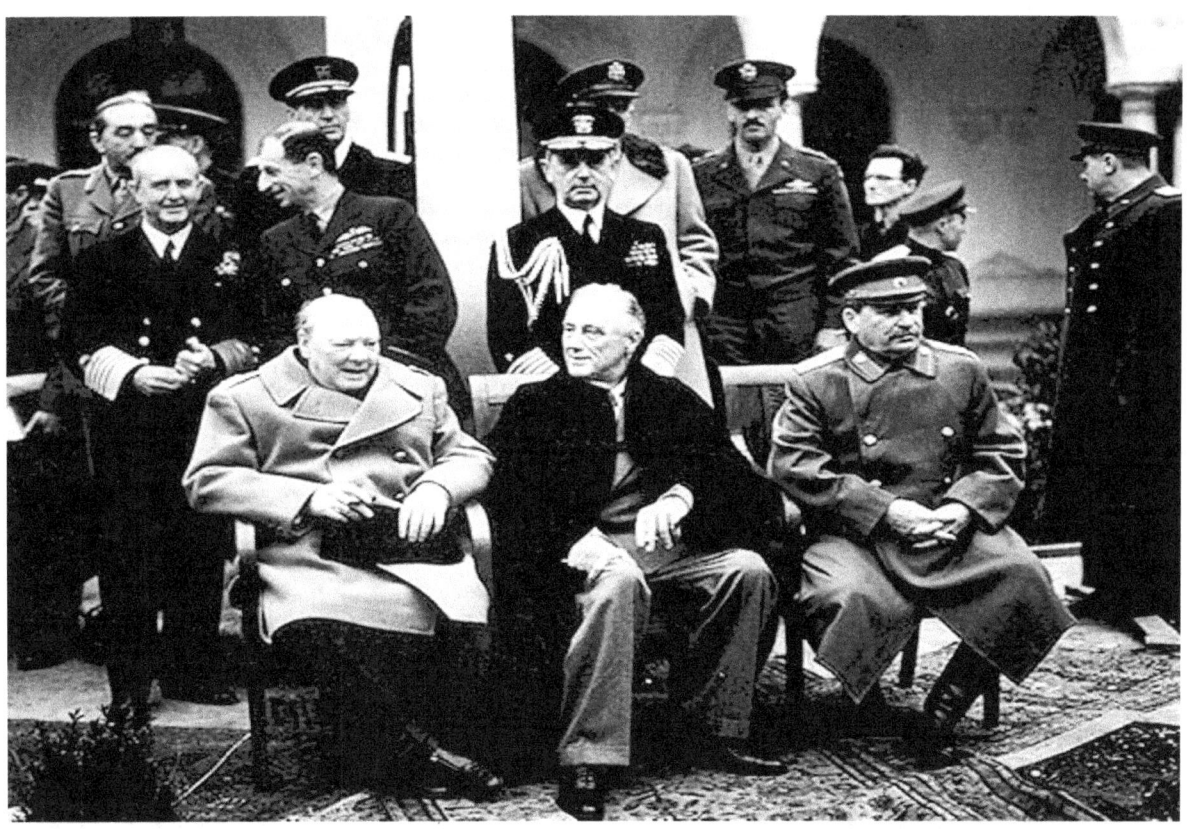

The Big Three: British Prime Minister Winston Churchill, U.S. President Franklin D. Roosevelt and Stalin at the Yalta Conference, February 1945.

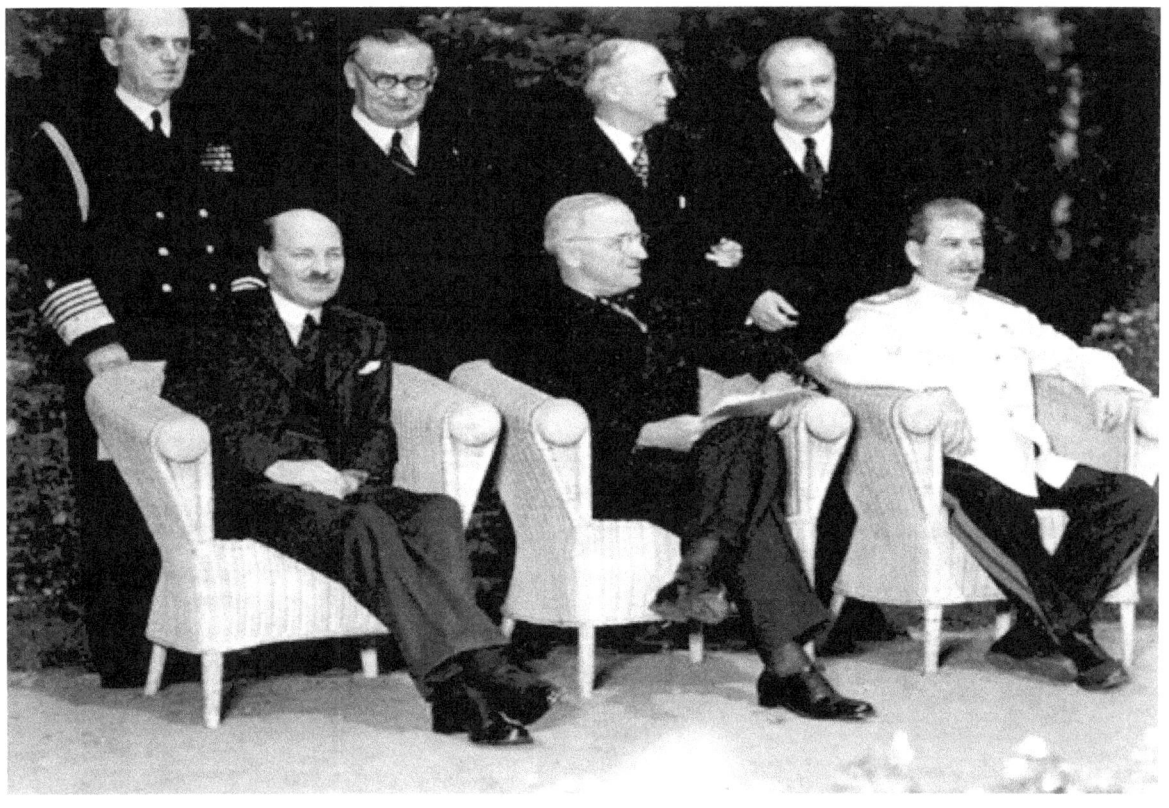

British Prime Minister Clement Attlee, U.S. President Harry S. Trumanand Joseph Stalin at the Potsdam Conference, July 1945.

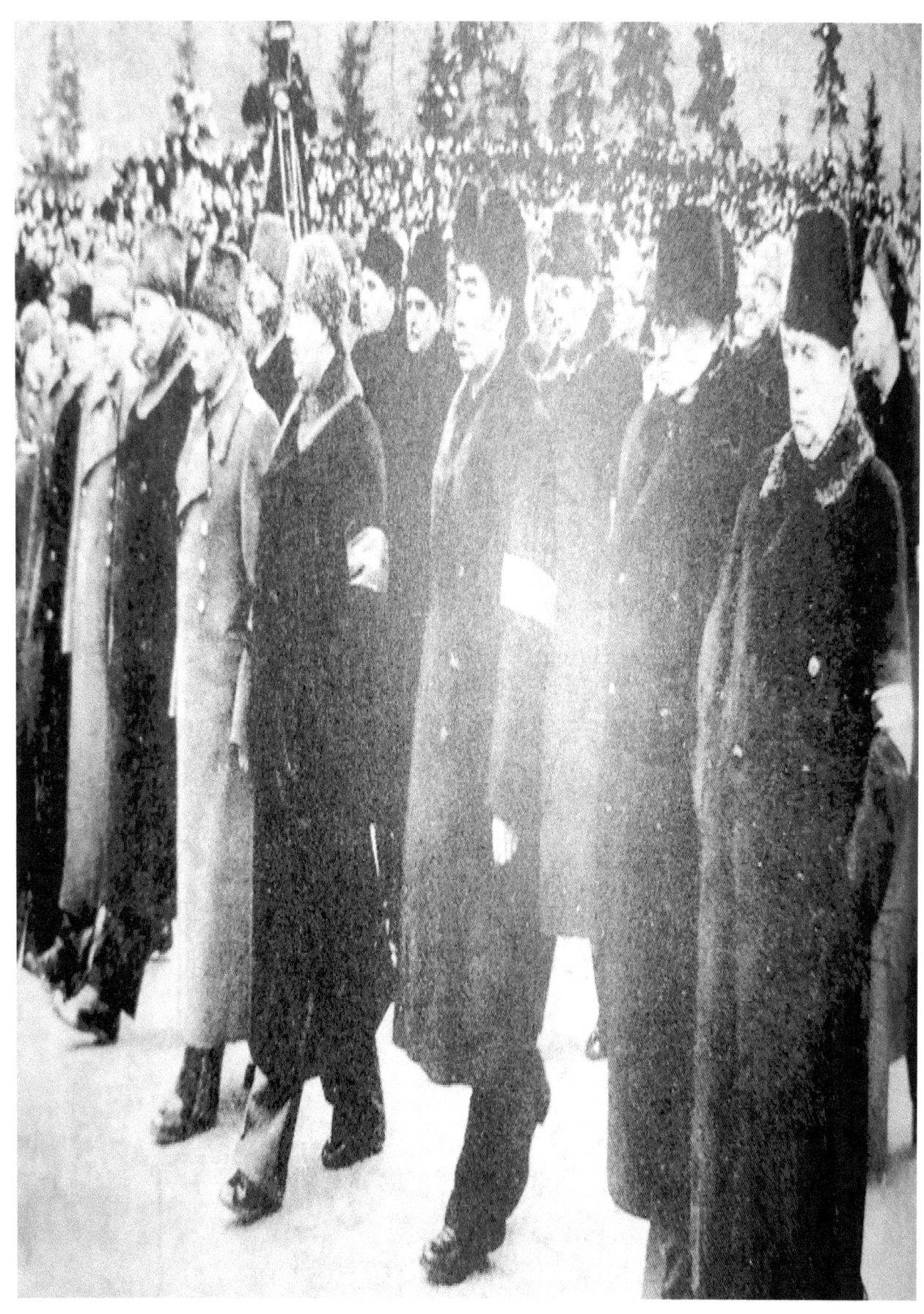

**Stalin's funeral. From right:<u>Khrushchev</u>, Beria, Chou En-
Lai,Malenkov, Voroshilov, Kaganovich, Bulganin, Molotov. (Sovfoto)**

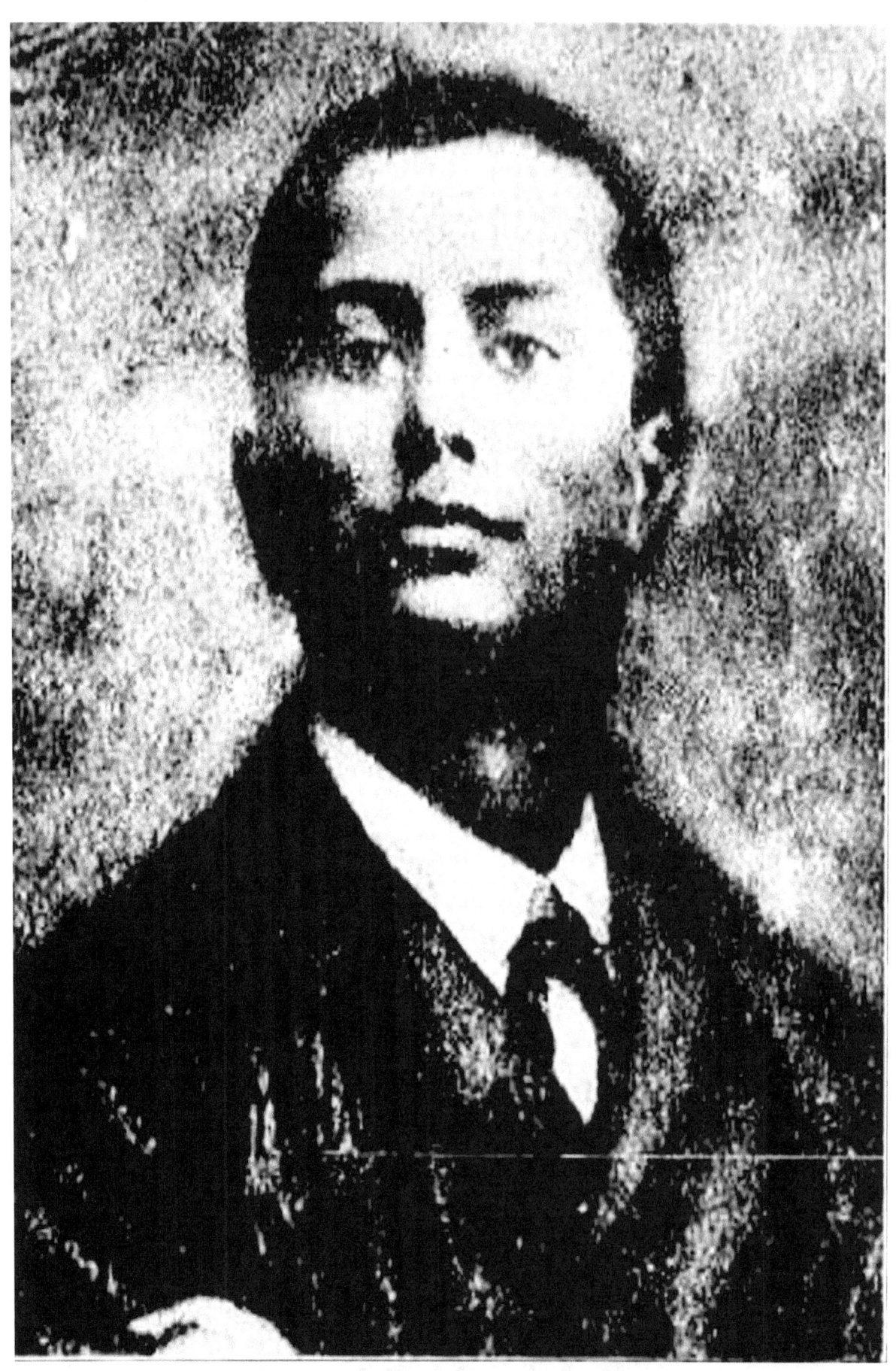

Benito Mussolini 1897 (14)

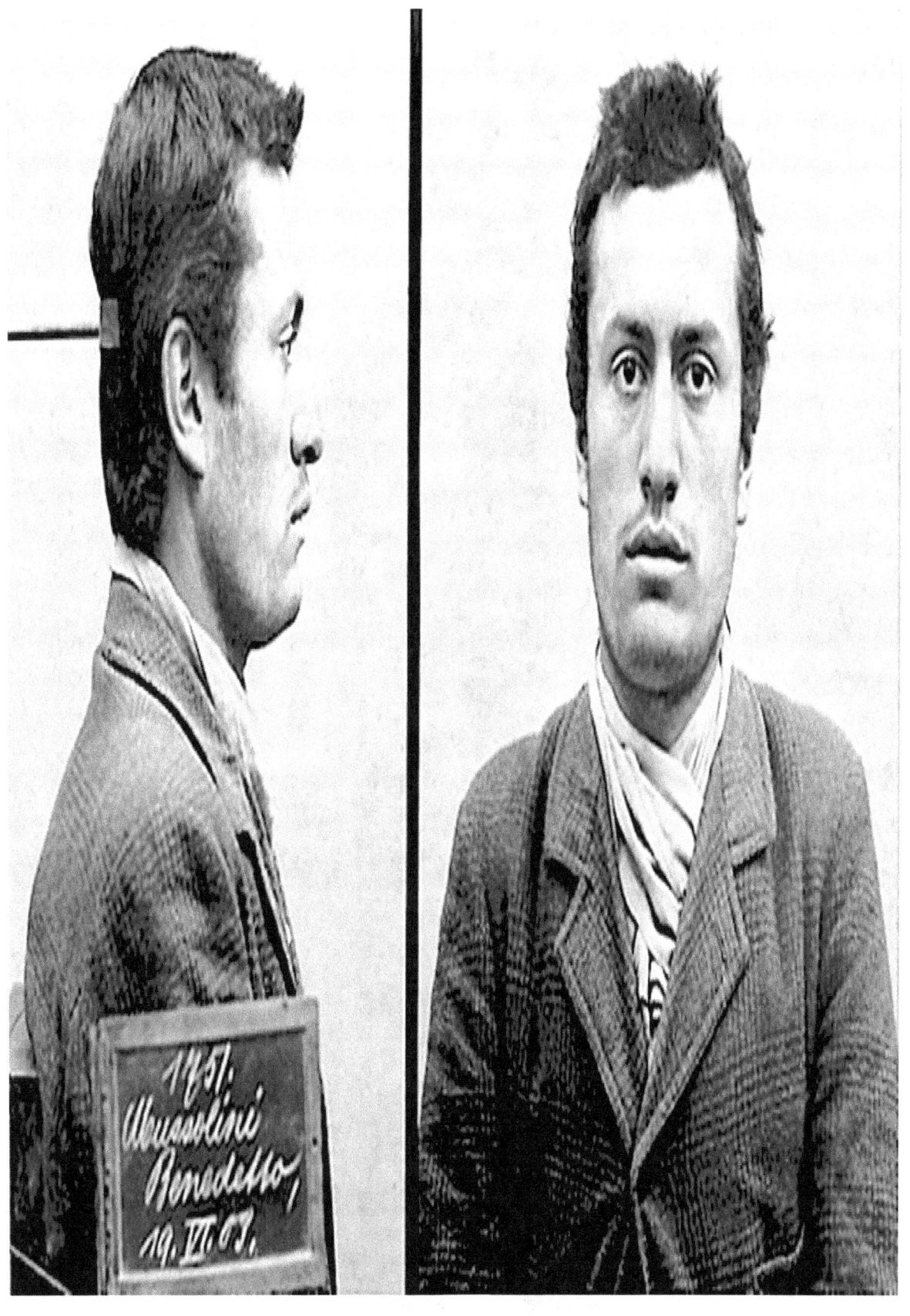

Mussolini's <u>booking photograph</u> following his arrest by Swiss police, 1903 (20)

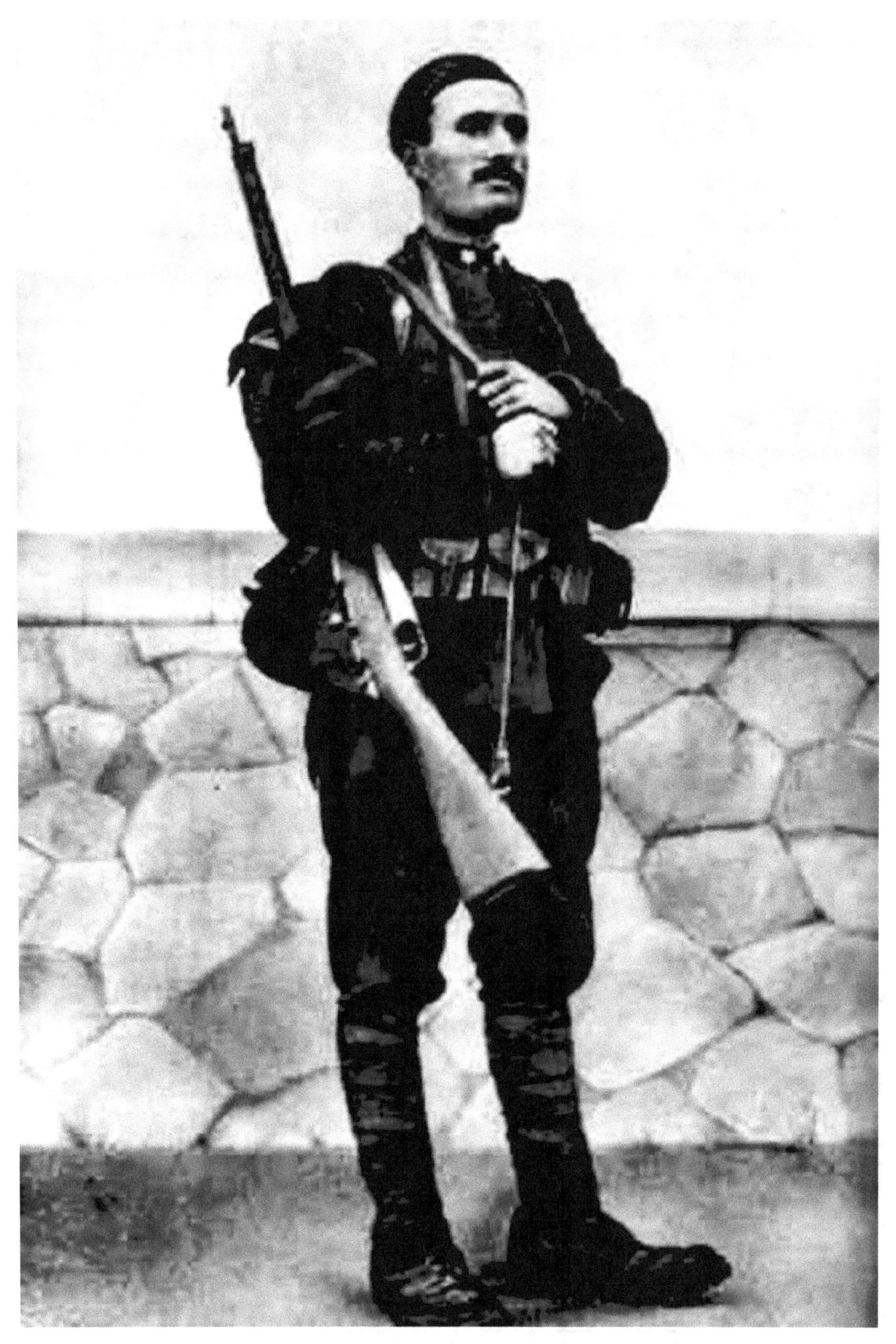

Benito Mussolini 1917 (34)

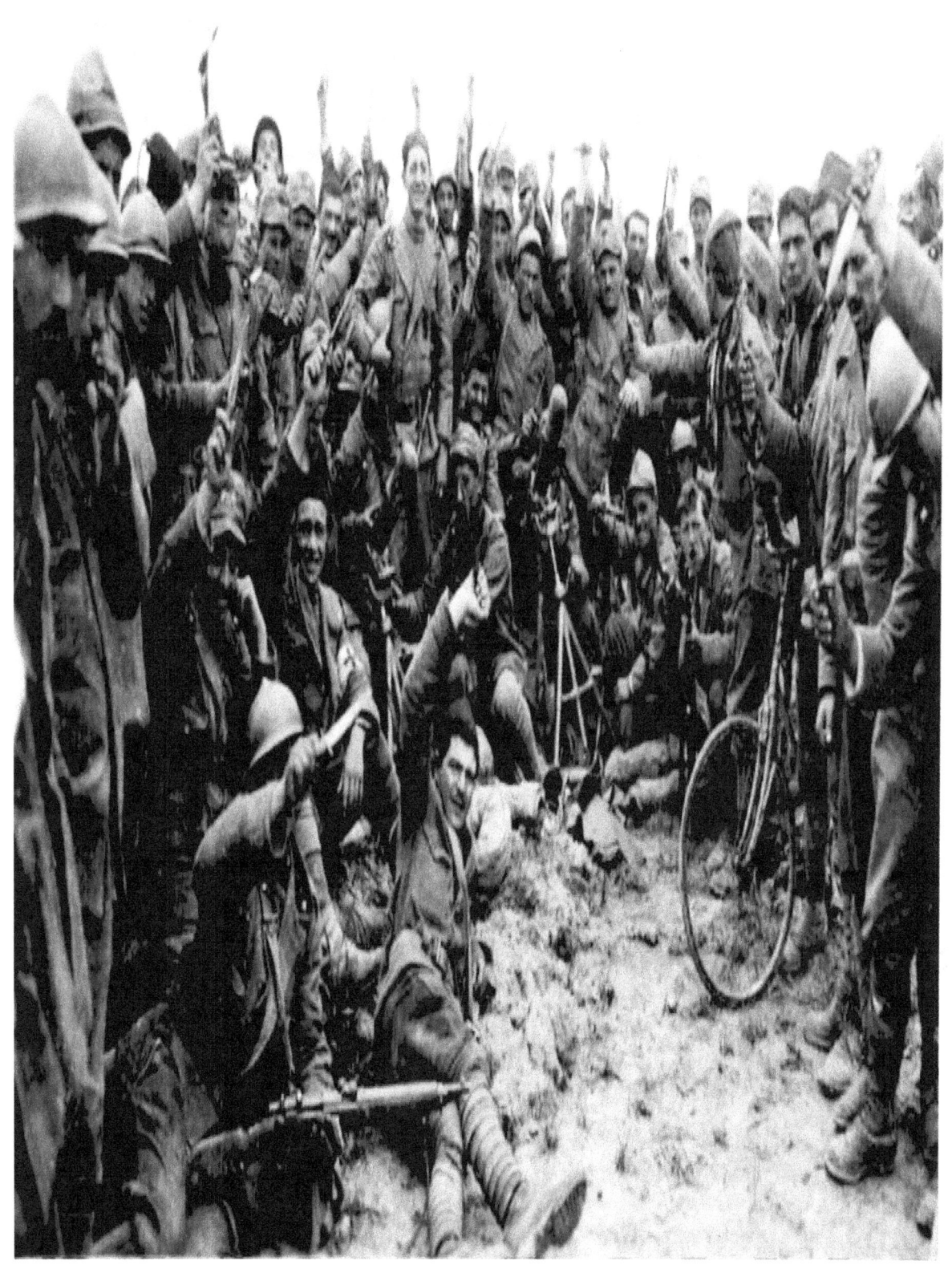

Members of Italy's *Arditi* corps in 1918

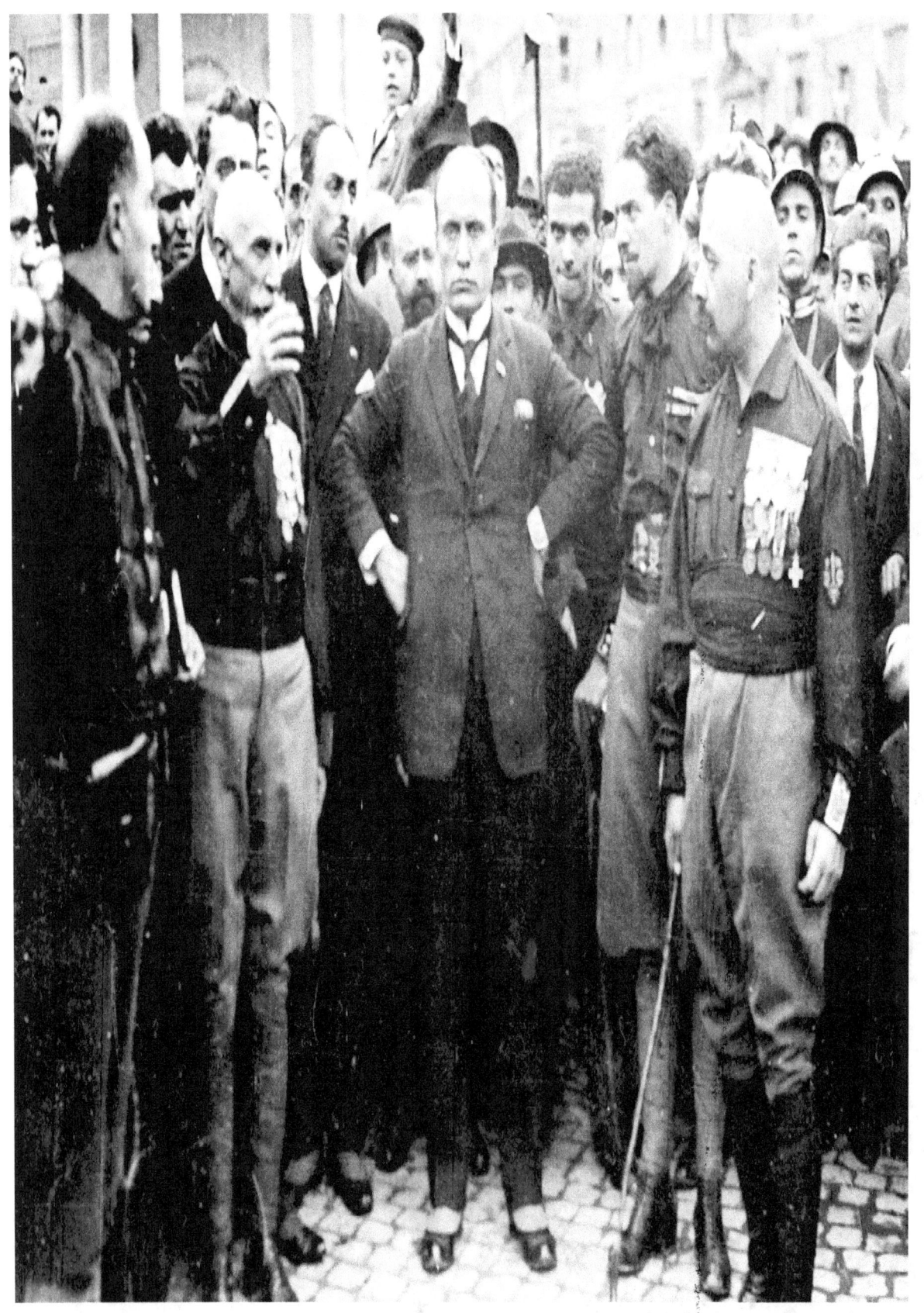

Mussolini and the *Quadrumviri* during the <u>March on Rome</u> in 1922 (39)

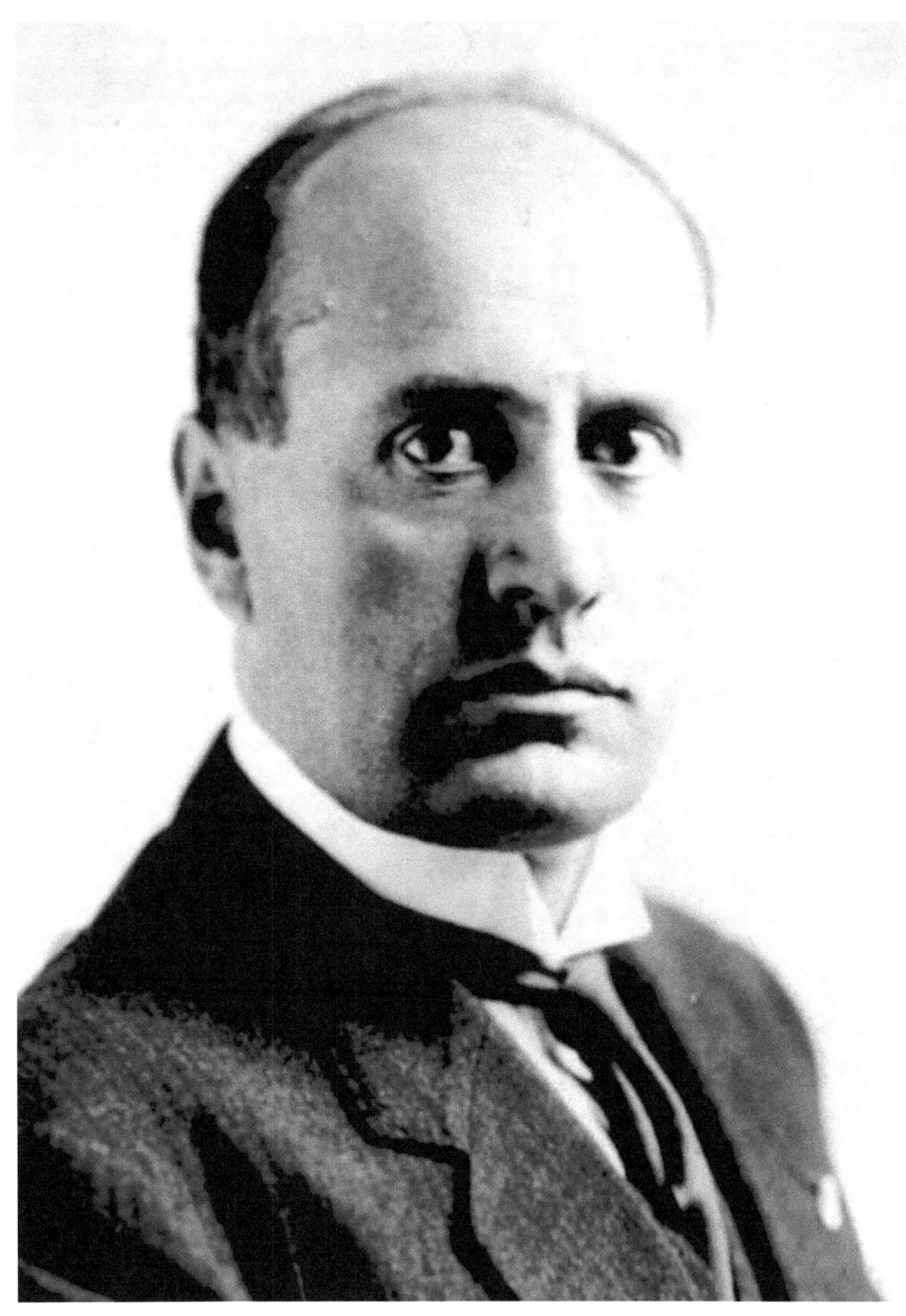

Mussolini during the 1920s, in his early years in power

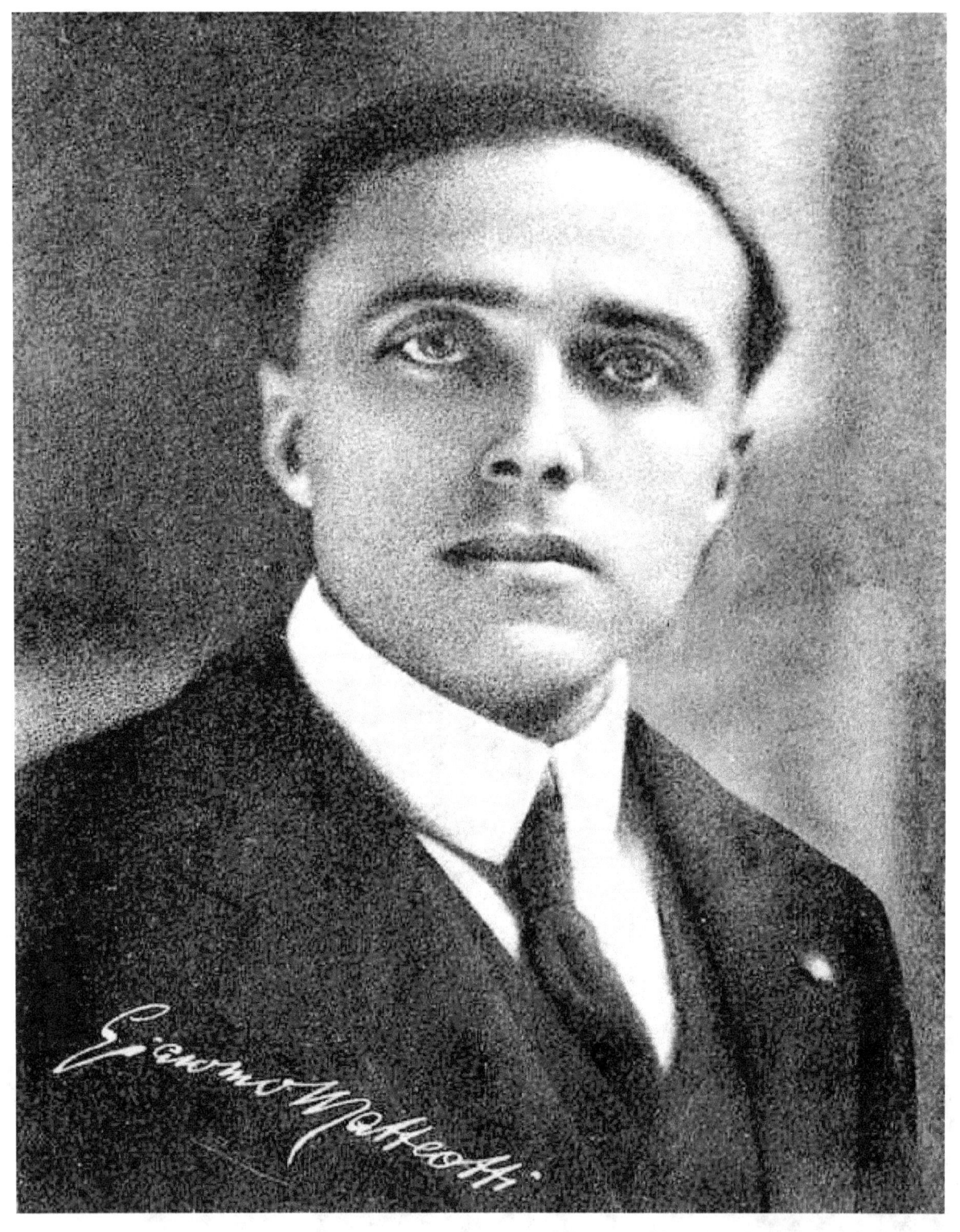

Socialist leader <u>Giacomo Matteotti</u> was murdered a few days after he openly denounced fascist violence during the 1924 elections.

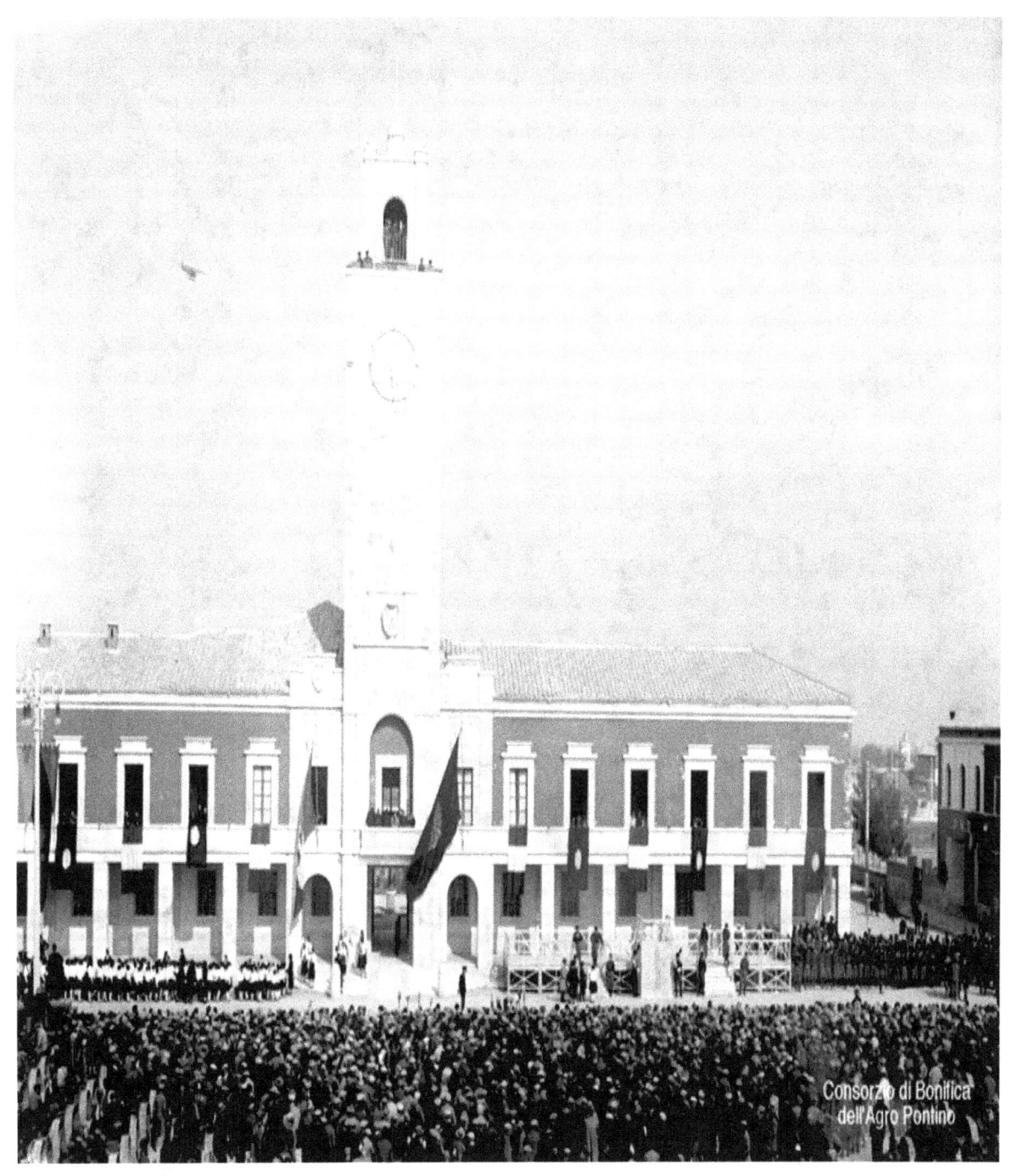

Mussolini launched several public construction programs and government initiatives throughout Italy to combat economic setbacks or unemployment levels. (The inauguration of Littoria in 1932), new agricultural town

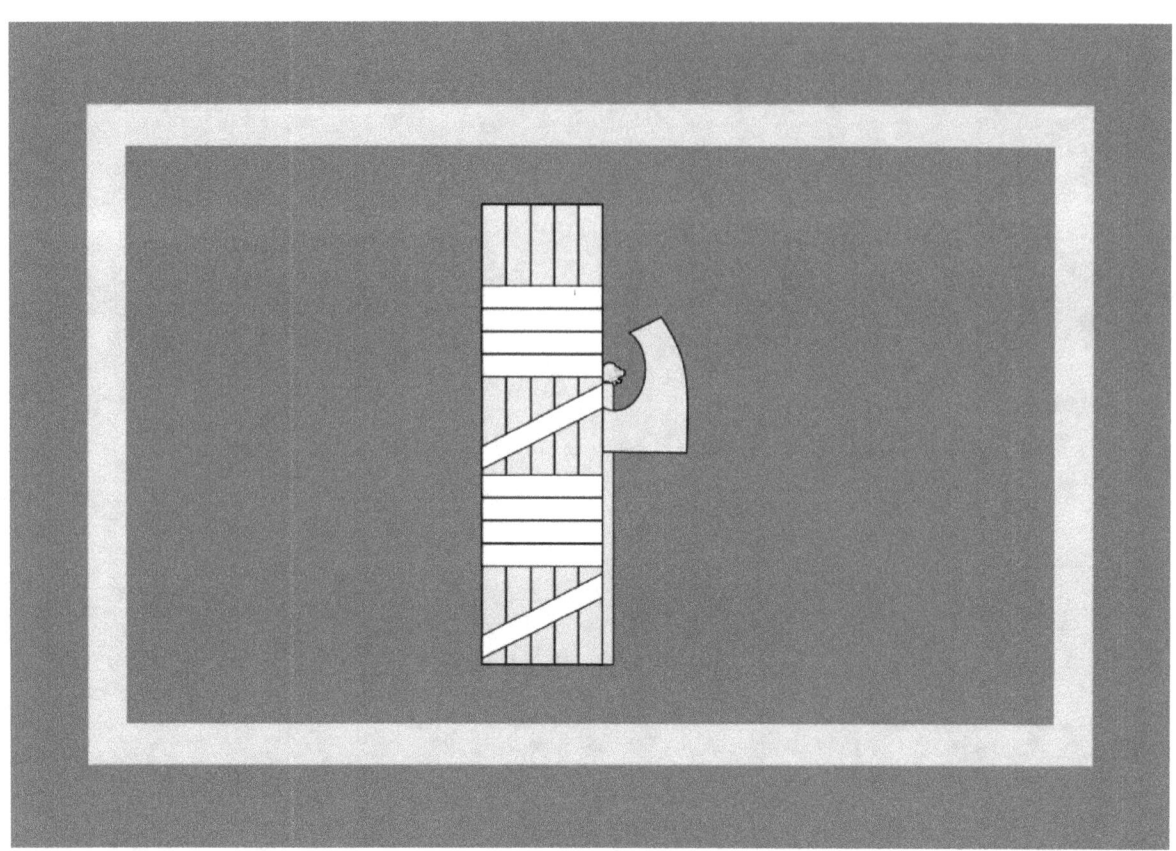

Mussolini's personal standard

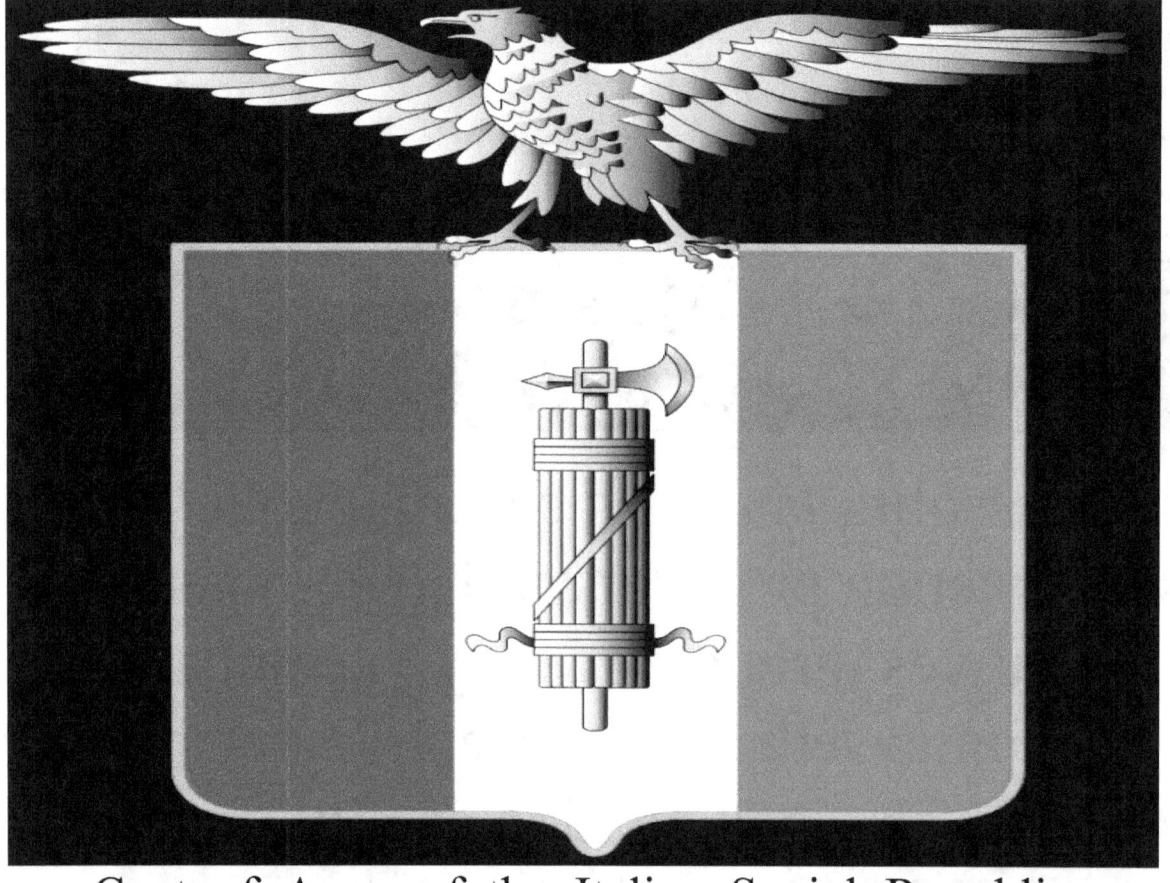

Coat_of_Arms_of_the_Italian_Social_Republic.

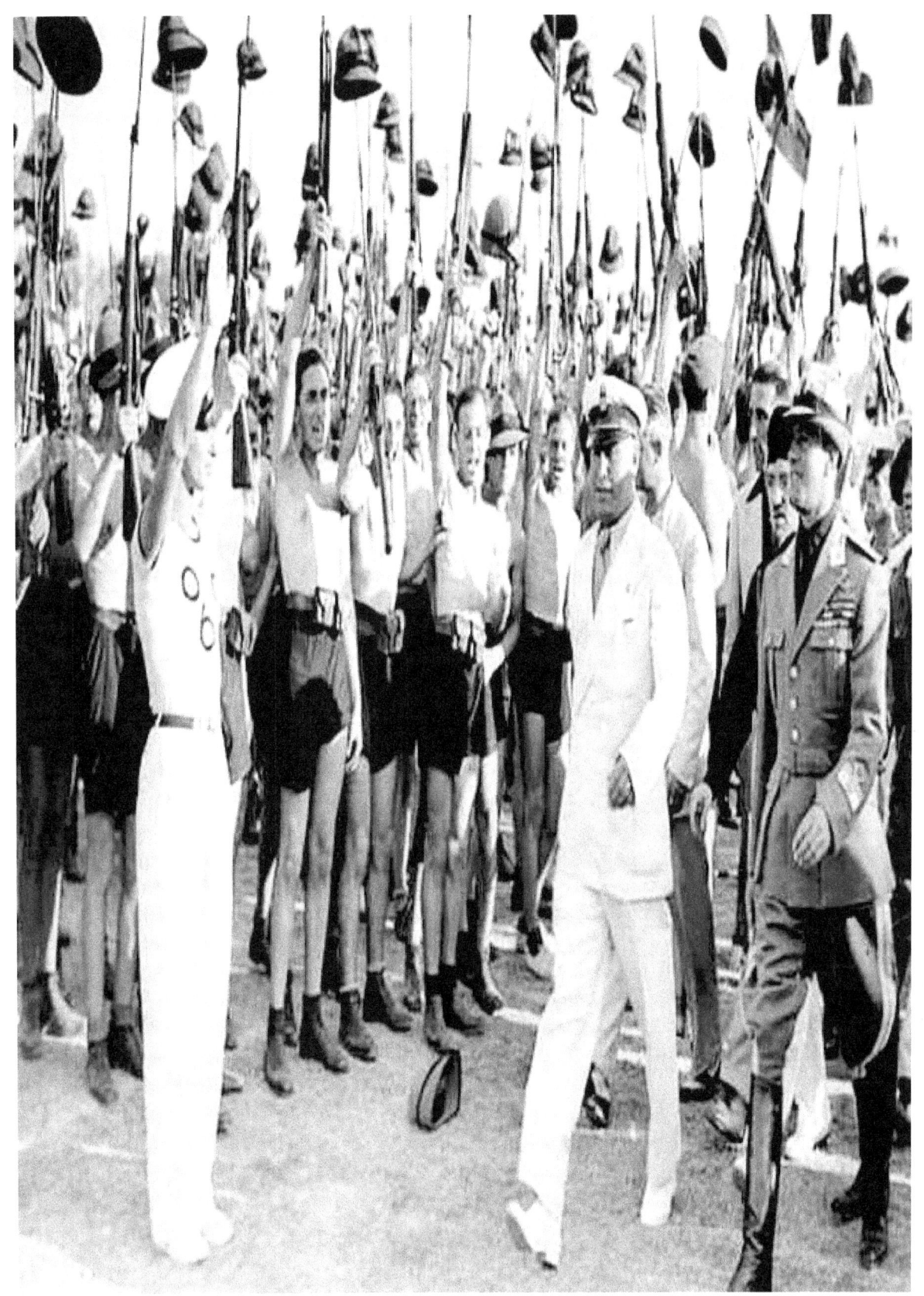

Benito Mussolini (52) and Fascist
Blackshirt youth in 1935

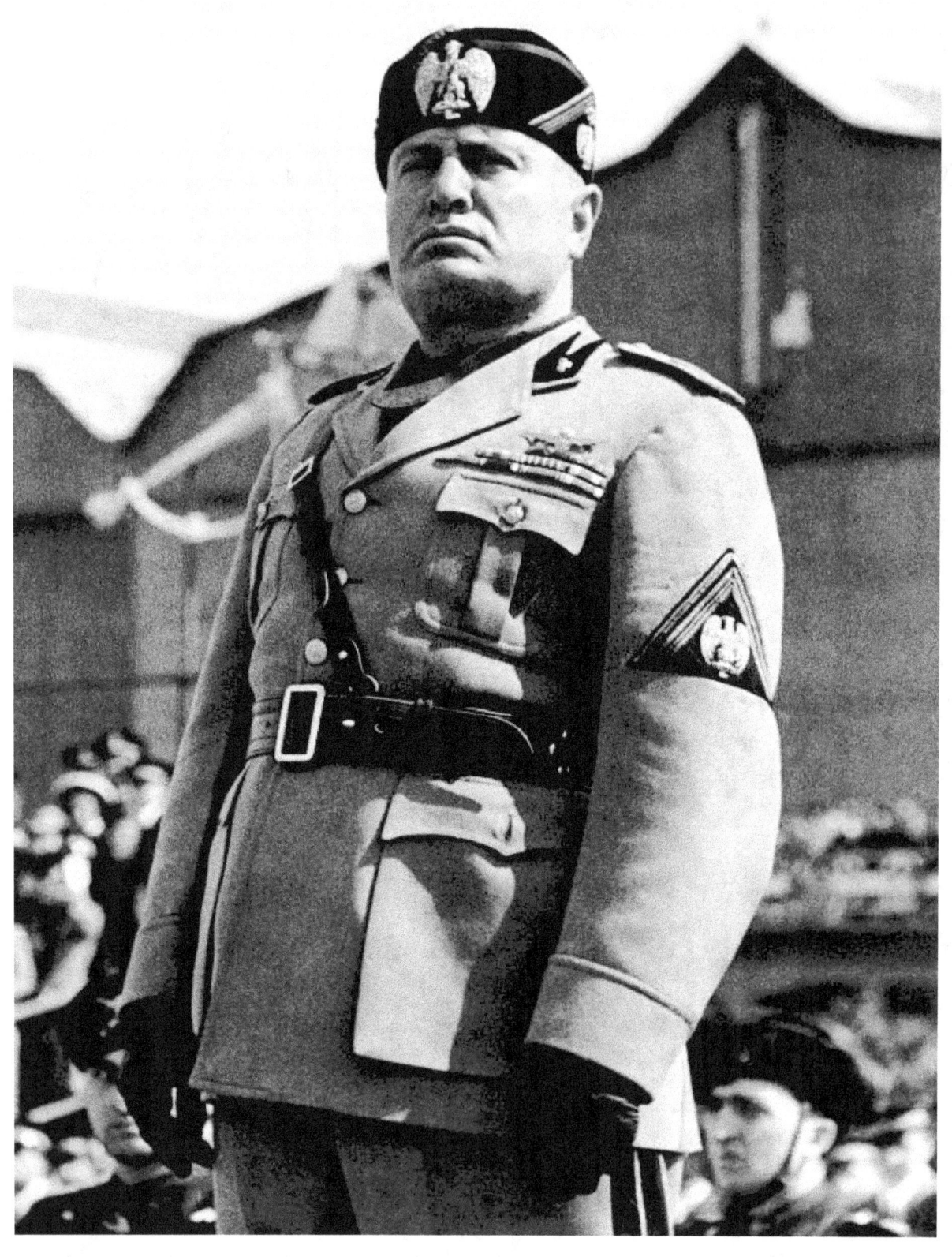

Benito Mussolini dressed in the fascist uniform

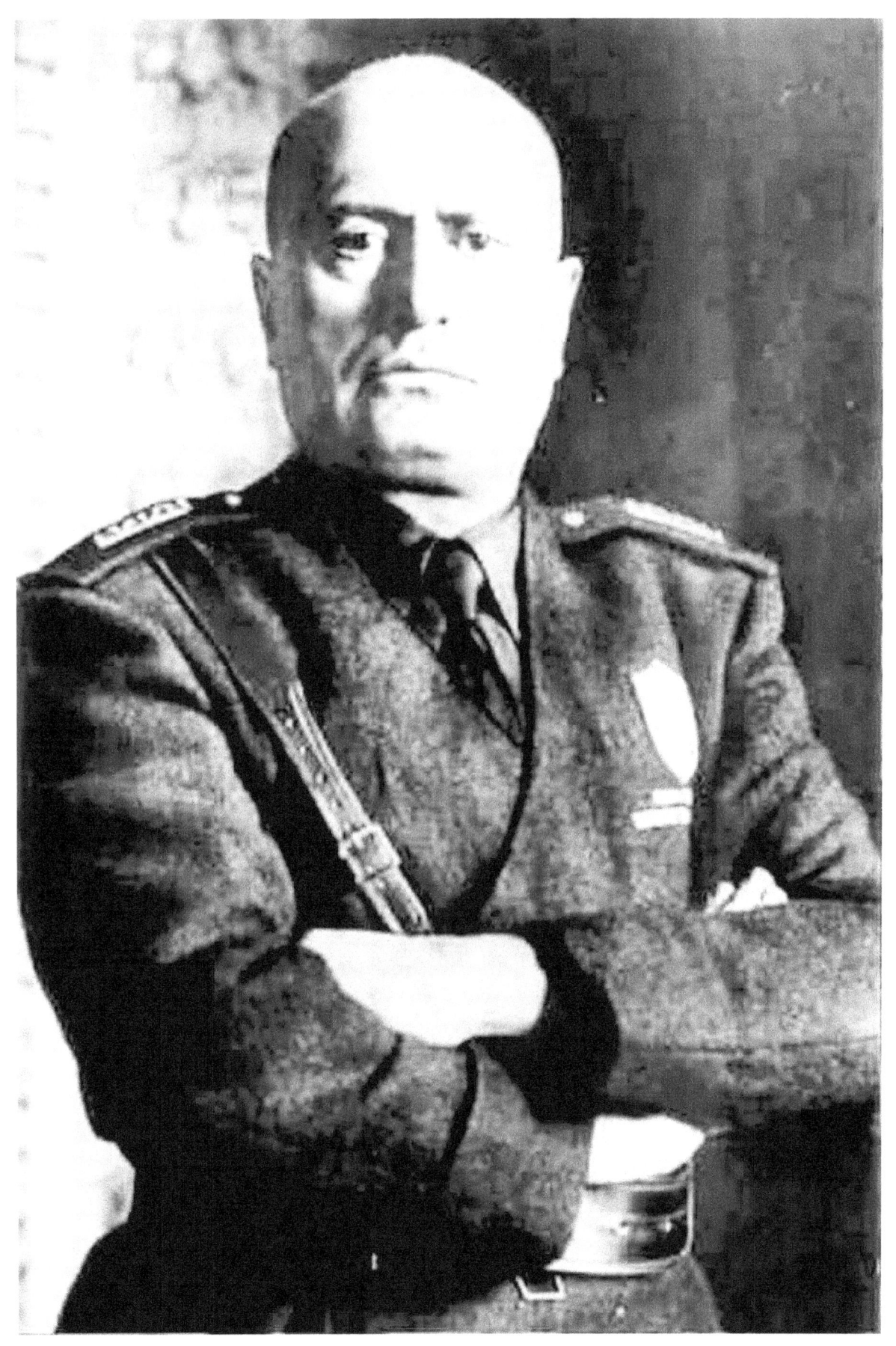

Mussolini in an official portrait

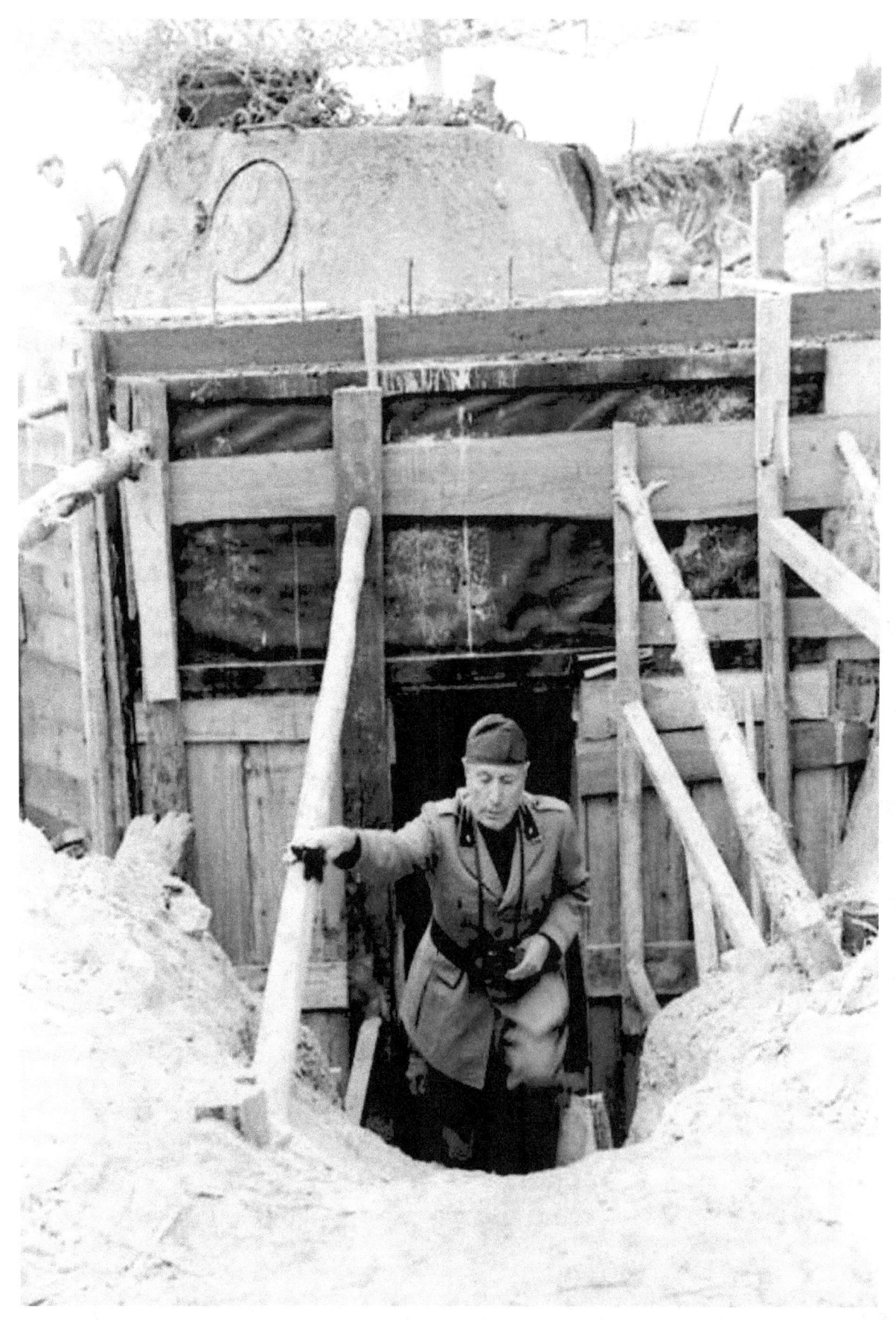

Mussolini (61) inspecting fortifications, 1944

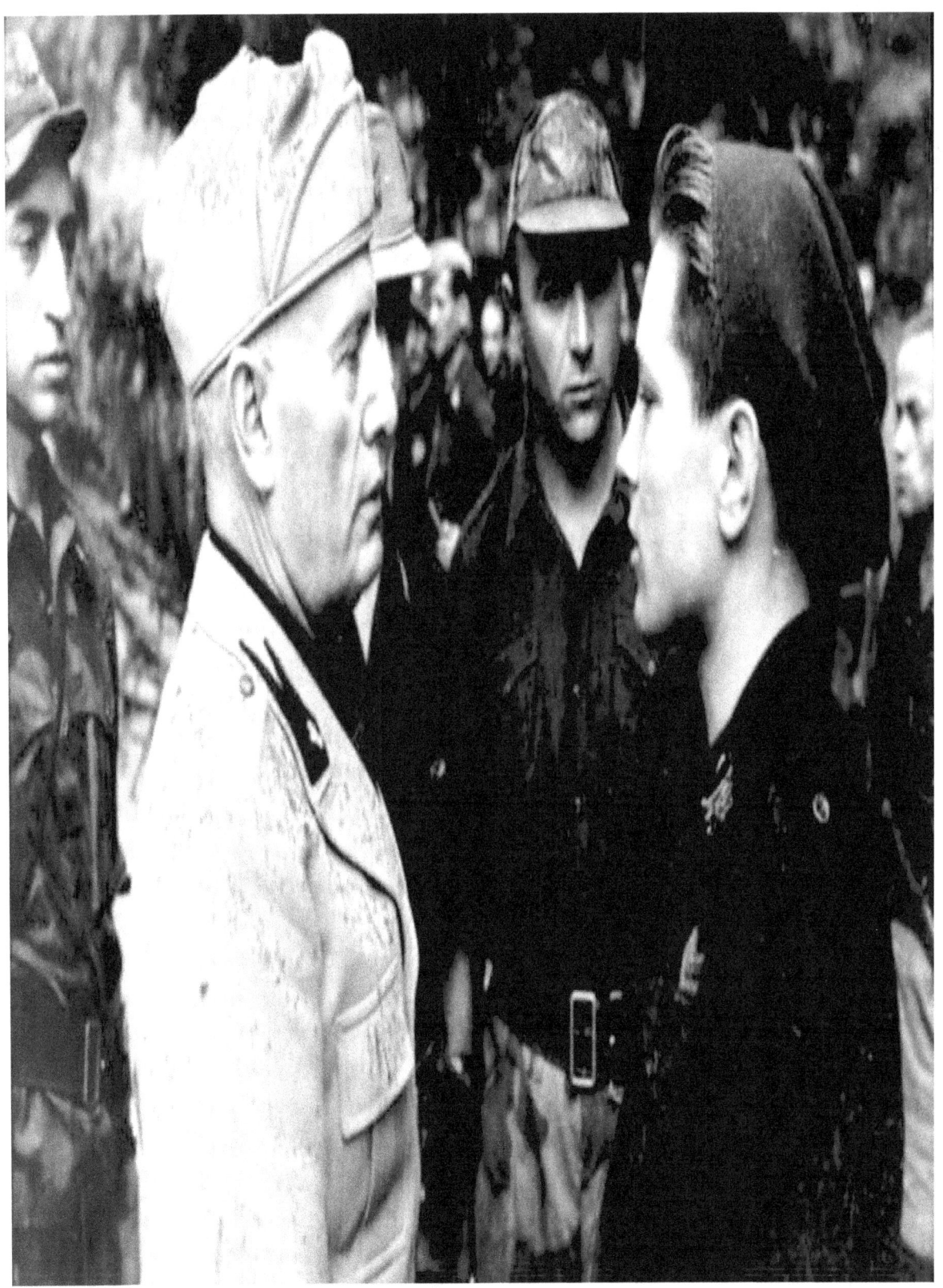

A rain-soaked Benito Mussolini reviewing adolescent soldiers in northern Italy, late 1944

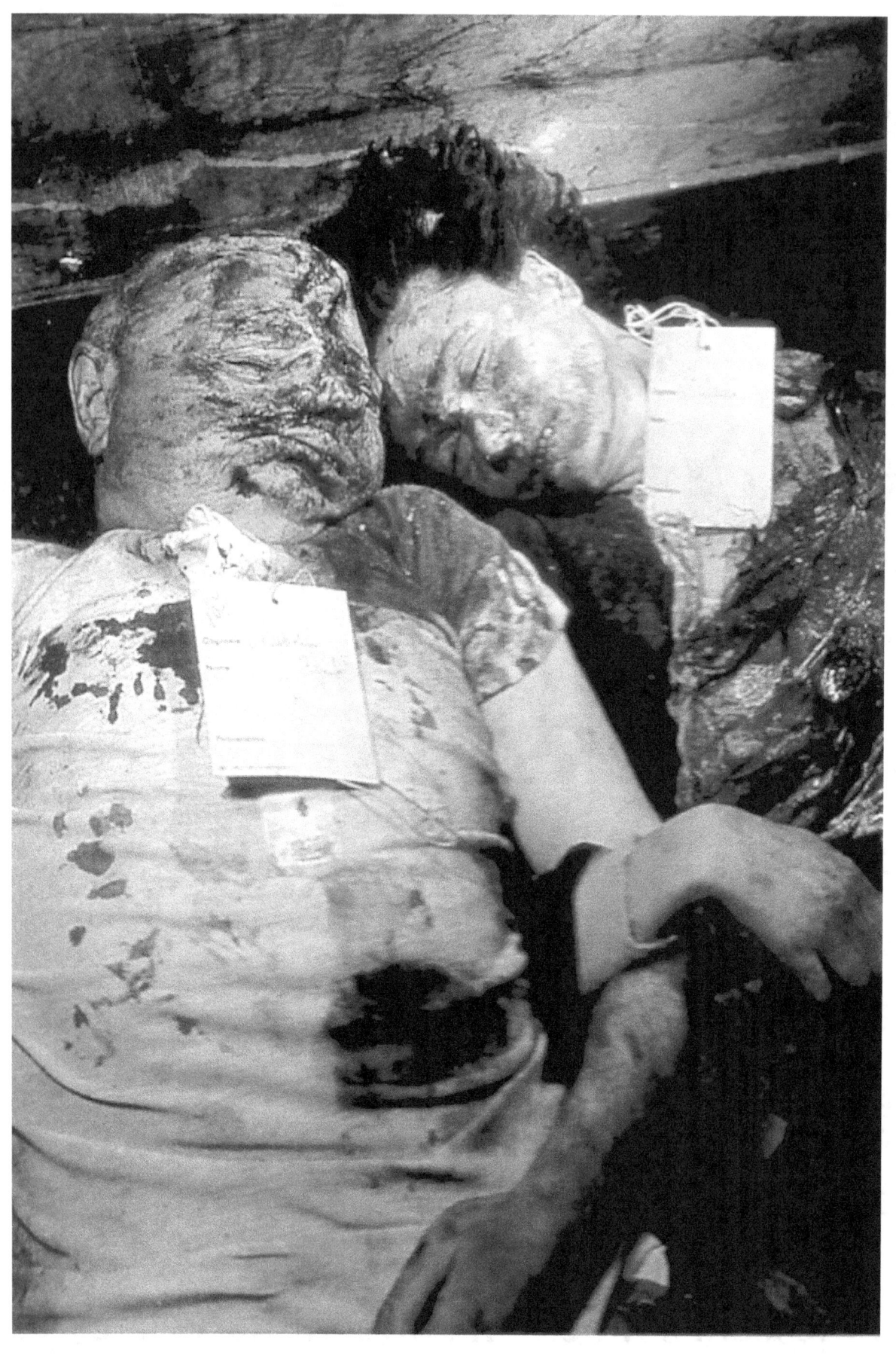

Dead Mussolini and Clara Petacci

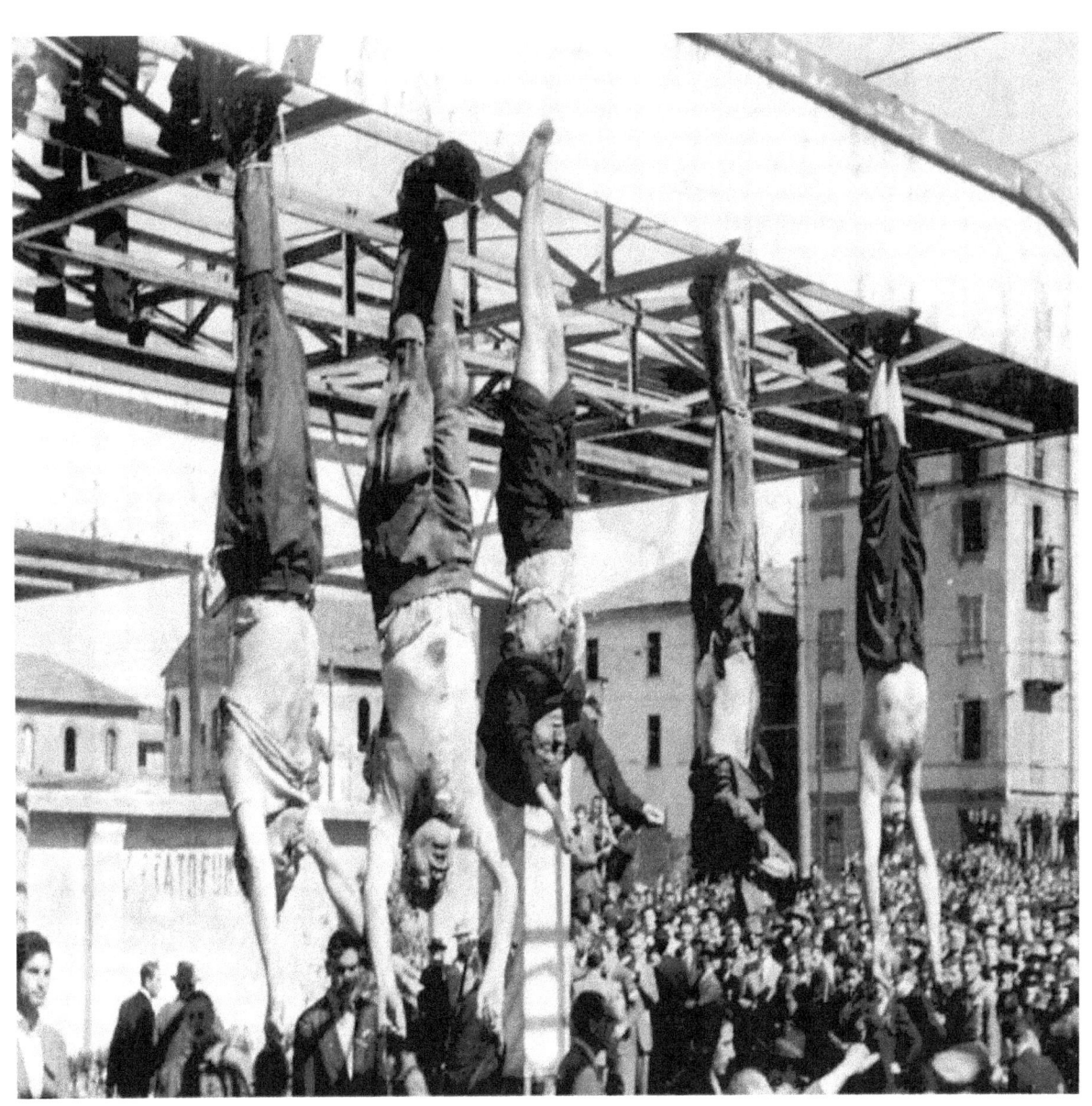

The corpse of Mussolini 62 (second from left) next to Petacci (middle) and other executed fascists in <u>Piazzale Loreto</u>, Milan

Here is Italy 1945
Welcome USA , Welcome. With Blue jean
Hamburger , coca cola and chips, Whiskey and
Rock and Roll , Muscle car, Curtiss , Martin ,
and Little boy

www.ingramcontent.com/pod-product-compliance
Lightning Source LLC
Chambersburg PA
CBHW081310180526

45170CB00007B/2642